Life, Liberty and the Pursuit of the Holy Spirit

A Study by
Amrita Philip

Edited by
Megha John Thomas

WESTBOW
PRESS®
A DIVISION OF THOMAS NELSON
& ZONDERVAN

WestBow Press books may be ordered through booksellers or by contacting:

WestBow Press
A Division of Thomas Nelson & Zondervan
1663 Liberty Drive
Bloomington, IN 47403
www.westbowpress.com
1 (866) 928-1240

Cover image by Sarah Sulek.

ISBN: 978-1-5127-6801-5 (sc)
ISBN: 978-1-5127-6802-2 (e)

Library of Congress Control Number: 2016920500

Print information available on the last page.

WestBow Press rev. date: 9/22/2017

FOREWORD

There are many different types of students, but the one that stands out amongst them in the eyes of God is the one who is a student of God's Word. The apostle Paul gives us this instruction in 2 Timothy 2:15, "Be diligent to present yourself approved to God, a worker who does not need to be ashamed, rightly dividing the word of truth." That verse comes directly to my mind when I think of Amrita. She has made becoming a student of God's word a priority in her life.

As the pastor of the church where she and her family have attended for many years, I have always admired and been inspired by her passion to rightly divide and teach God's word. In this book, she has allowed her stewardship of God's Word, her wealth of knowledge and diligent study, to travel through a pen from her heart and land on paper in a way that will open the eyes of all to the powerful and needed help of the Holy Spirit in our everyday life.

Jesus told His followers that it was to our advantage that He go away, so the Holy Spirit could come. From cover to cover, Amrita walks the reader through what that advantage is for our life. I'm thrilled about the wealth of revelation that this book contains and for the many lives that will be richly impacted. We all need help in life, and the Holy Spirit was sent to be that Helper.

Thank you, Amrita, for all your diligence and the sacrifice you made to bring these timeless truths to the Body of Christ. Our lives will be better because of it.

Rusty Greer
Lead Pastor
The Worship Center, Houston

PREFACE

This book is a result of a Life group study held at our home. I had no idea it would span four years! With each lesson, we received another revelation and a burst of life. My hope is that the reader will be blessed with the same experience.

As we pursue the Holy Spirit through the pages of this book, may we receive the life and liberty that comes only when we make Him Lord of our lives.

ACKNOWLEDGMENTS

I would like to thank:

- My husband, Vino, without whom this book would not exist. You have supported me all the way. If it were left to me, these pages would be stuffed in a drawer and eventually trashed during a fit of spring cleaning. You organized the material and had the foresight to put it all in a binder!

- My parents, who were not afraid to leave their traditions to raise us in a Spirit-filled environment. They taught us to honor both the Spirit and the Word.

- Pastor Dil Kumar, who showed me just how close we can walk with the Holy Spirit.

- Pastor Rusty Greer, whose sermons inspired and challenged me to do what I considered impossible – actually write this book. Your sermon, "It seemed good", gave me the *rhema* word that convinced me that this was a God-thing. Along the way, I got discouraged and stopped writing. Your "Unstoppable" series put me back on track.

- Megha, my editor, who spent countless hours on my manuscript. You came to my aid when I was tearing my hair out. It will take several bottles of brinjal pickle to pay you back.

- Carolyn, for guiding me through the arduous process of proofing the manuscript. Thanks for helping me redraft the chapter on wisdom and cheering me on. We will celebrate over Nutella crepes.

- David, for helping out with edits even with your busy schedule. You made it legit!

CONTENTS

SECTION 1

WHO HE IS

WHO IS THE HOLY SPIRIT?

Have you ever wondered who the Holy Spirit is? How can He be a part of our lives today? Why do we need Him? Is He just some vapor or smoke that was last seen in the book of Acts? Let us look at Him from every angle in Scripture so that we may know Him more.

WHO IS THE HOLY SPIRIT?

The Spirit of the Lord is GOD. He is a PERSON. The Bible personifies the Holy Spirit as a HIM, not an IT. He is the third person of the Trinity; not lower in position, but one with the Father and with Jesus Christ. He is not a vapor or a ghost like the fictional character, Casper . He is a tangible person with an awesome and sweet presence. He is the most powerful being, yet the gentlest person.

NAMES OF THE HOLY SPIRIT

The Holy Spirit has been described by His numerous characteristics and personas in the KJV – the Spirit of the Lord (Isa. 40:13-14); Spirit of God (Gen. 1:2); Holy Ghost (Luke 1:35); Spirit of Adoption (Rom. 8:15); Spirit of Christ (Rom. 8:9); Comforter (John 14:16); Spirit of Truth (John 14:17); Spirit of Holiness (Rom. 1:4); Spirit of Life (Rom. 8:2); Spirit of Promise (Eph. 1:13); Spirit of Grace (Heb. 10:29), among others.

IN THE BEGINNING

> "Now the earth was formless and empty, darkness covered the surface of the watery depths, and the Spirit of God was hovering over the surface of the waters." (Gen. 1:2, HCSB)

The word 'hovering' paints a picture of a hen brooding over her eggs. Before God moved over the waters, there was darkness and desolation. God begins His marvelous work of creation, bringing in light, beauty, and purpose to the otherwise chaotic world.

Before a great work of God comes to pass in our individual worlds, we need the Holy Spirit to brood over us as well.

> "And the angel answered and said unto her, "The Holy Ghost shall come upon thee, and the power of the Highest shall overshadow thee: therefore, also that holy thing which shall be born of thee shall be called the Son of God."" (Luke 1:35, HCSB)

When the Holy Spirit overshadowed Mary, He was making the way for the Word to become flesh and dwell among us. This is the greatest of all miracles. Luke 1:79 tells us how Jesus came to the world to shine light on those that live in darkness and in the shadow of death.

We need the Holy Spirit to help us connect with God. We need the light of the Holy Spirit to help us see how we live.

SALVATION

The Holy Spirit brings us to salvation in Jesus, and we are adopted as God's children into His family.

How can we experience salvation? In Acts 16:30-31, the Philippian jailor asks Paul and Silas the question, "What must I do to be saved?" and they said, "Believe in the Lord Jesus and you and your household shall be saved."

> "But to all who did receive Him, He gave them the right to be children of God, to those who believe in His name..." (John 1:12, HCSB)

> "⁹If you confess with your mouth, "Jesus is Lord," and believe in your heart that God raised Him from the dead, you will be saved. ¹⁰One believes with the heart, resulting in righteousness, and one confesses with the mouth, resulting in salvation." (Rom. 10:9-10, HCSB)

Once we receive Jesus as the only Lord and Savior, believe in His name and in His resurrection by God, and confess this fact with our mouth, we will be made righteous by the cleansing power of the blood of Jesus. There is no other name under heaven by which we are saved.

> "For you did not receive a spirit of slavery to fall back into fear, but you received the Spirit of adoption, by whom we cry out, "*Abba*, Father!" (Rom. 8:15, HCSB)

The Holy Spirit brings us to salvation in Jesus, and we are adopted as God's children into His family.

> "¹⁶The Spirit Himself testifies together with our spirit that we are God's children, ¹⁷and if children, also heirs – heirs of God and coheirs with Christ – seeing that we suffer with Him so that we may also be glorified with Him." (Rom. 8:16-17, HCSB)

We cannot become God's children on our own merit.

> "When you heard the message of truth, the gospel of your salvation, and when you believed in Him, you were also sealed with the promised Holy Spirit." (Eph. 1:13, HCSB)

> "You, however, are not in the flesh, but in the Spirit, since the Spirit of God lives in you. But if anyone does not have the Spirit of Christ, he does not belong to Him." (Rom. 8:9, HCSB)

"¹⁶And I will ask the Father, and He will give you another Counselor to be with you forever. ¹⁷He is the Spirit of truth. The world is unable to receive Him because it doesn't see Him or know Him. But you do know Him, because He remains with you and will be in you." (John 14:16-17, HCSB)

We may not be able to see the Holy Spirit, but that need not stop us from experiencing His presence and communing with Him.

THE TRANSFORMING WORK OF THE HOLY SPIRIT

The Holy Spirit alone can change a sinner into a new creation in Christ Jesus. God commands us in 1 Peter 1:15 to "Be holy as I am holy." We cannot make ourselves holy, as our own righteousness is as a filthy rag, as depicted in Isaiah 64:6. The Holy Spirit will make us holy. Romans 1:4 refers to Him as the 'Spirit of Holiness'.

THE WORKS OF THE HOLY SPIRIT

WASHES AND CLEANSES US

> "...But you were washed, you were sanctified, you were justified in the name of the Lord Jesus Christ and by the Spirit of our God." (1 Cor. 6:11, HCSB)

> "...the blood of Jesus His Son cleanses us from all sin." (1 John 1:7, HCSB)

> "If we confess our sins, He is faithful and righteous to forgive us our sins and to cleanse us from all unrighteousness." (1 John 1:9, HCSB)

> "Though your sins are like scarlet, they will be as white as snow; though they are as red as crimson, they will be like wool." (Isa. 1:18, HCSB)

As the familiar song goes, "Are you washed in the blood of the lamb?", Leviticus 14:4 -7 talks about how one bird is killed under running water, and the other is dipped in its blood and set free. This is symbolic of Jesus being killed in our place and us being washed in the blood of Jesus and being set free. This was also part of the ritual to cleanse a leper. Here, leprosy was equated to sin. The sinner, like the leper is cleansed when he is sprinkled with the blood of the slain Lamb.

SANCTIFIES US

The Holy Spirit and the blood of Jesus sanctify us. Sanctification means to make holy, set apart as sacred, consecrate, to purify or free from sin.

> "But we must always thank God for you, brothers loved by the Lord, because from the beginning God has chosen you for salvation through sanctification by the Spirit and through belief in the truth." (2 Thess. 2:13, HCSB)

> "...according to the foreknowledge of God the Father and set apart by the Spirit for obedience and for sprinkling with the blood of Jesus Christ." (1 Pet. 1:2, HCSB)

JUSTIFIES US

This is the act of God whereby we are made free from the guilt and penalty of sin. It is easy to remember the phrase, "Just as if he has not sinned". In Leviticus 16:8-10, the Lord's lot falls on one of two goats that is killed as a sin offering. The other goat is sent away into the wilderness. We deserved to die, but the Lord has laid on Him the iniquity of us all, and we escape the wages of sin, which is death.

EMANCIPATES US

> "Now the Lord is the Spirit, and where the Spirit of the Lord is, there is freedom."
> (2 Cor. 3:17, HCSB)

The bird and the goat in the books of Leviticus were both set free. We have been set free from sin and death to live in obedience and serve God.

RECEIVES US

Mankind was alienated from God because of Adam's sin. Jesus reconciled man to God, and now through the Holy Spirit, we can approach the Father without fear.

> "For through Him we both have access by one Spirit unto the Father." (Eph. 2:18, HCSB)

ABIDES IN US

We were made to be inhabited by the Holy Spirit. This is why the unbeliever has a feeling of emptiness. Once a man is born again, he becomes a temple for God. This is a great mystery, for even the heavens cannot contain Him, yet He chooses to live in us.

> "Don't you yourselves know that you are God's sanctuary and that the Spirit of God lives in you?" (1 Cor. 3:16, HCSB)

> "¹⁹So then you are no longer foreigners and strangers, but fellow citizens with the saints, and members of God's household, ²⁰built on the foundation of the apostles and prophets, with Christ Jesus Himself as the cornerstone. ²¹The whole building, being put together by Him, grows into a holy sanctuary in the Lord. ²²You also are being built together for God's dwelling in the Spirit." (Eph. 2:19-22, HCSB)

UNIFIES US

Before Christ, the Jews alone were part of the family of God. All others were foreigners to the covenant. Jesus has broken down this wall of separation so that all who believe in Him are part of His body, the church.

"For we were all baptized by one Spirit into one body – whether Jews or Greeks, whether slaves or free – and we were all made to drink of one Spirit..." (1 Cor. 12:13, HCSB)

COUNSELS US

"You sent Your good Spirit to instruct them..." (Neh. 9:20, HCSB)

God gives His people counsel through the word and the Holy Spirit. He is called the Counselor. We have the choice to obey or refuse His counsel.

"But the Counselor, the Holy Spirit – the Father will send Him in My name – will teach you all things and remind you of everything I have told you." (John 14:26, HCSB)

In Acts 8:26-39, a eunuch reads the scripture, but is unable to understand its depth. In Acts 8:30-31, (HCSB) Philip asks him the question, "Do you understand what you're reading?" The eunuch replies, "How can I, unless someone guides me?" Philip sat by his side and shared the good news about Jesus with him. If we read the Bible without the Spirit, we are like this eunuch, unable to understand. If we ask the Holy Spirit for understanding, He will sit beside us, like Philip did, and expound the scripture at our level, so we can see Jesus in the scripture.

"The anointing you received from Him remains in you, and you don't need anyone to teach you. Instead, His anointing teaches you about all things and is true and is not a lie; just as He has taught you, remain in Him." (1 John 2: 27, HCSB)

The Holy Spirit will never tell us anything that contradicts God's word. He always speaks that which glorifies Christ. He speaks the truth. The Spirit testifies of Christ.

"[13]When the Spirit of truth comes; He will guide you into all the truth. For He will not speak on His own, but He will speak whatever He hears. He will also declare to you what is to come. [14] He will glorify Me, because He will take from what is Mine and declare it to you." (John 16:13-14, HCSB)

LEADS US

As in Luke 2: 25, Simeon was waiting for the Messiah to come. As the Spirit led him to see Jesus, He will lead us to see Jesus and the salvation that is found only in Him.

"When the Counselor comes, the One I will send to you from the Father – the Spirit of truth who proceeds from the Father – He will testify about Me." (John 15:26, HCSB)

In summary, the Holy Spirit is multi-faceted: He guides us in all truth; He will not speak of Himself but testifies of Christ; He brings to remembrance the words of Christ; He will speak whatever he hears from Jesus; He will show us things to come; He glorifies Jesus; and He will abide with us forever.

HOW CAN WE RECEIVE THE HOLY SPIRIT?

Galatians 3:2 shows us that we cannot receive the Spirit by doing the doing the works of the law, but through the hearing of faith. Galatians 3:14 indicates we can receive the promise of the Spirit through faith.

STEPS TO RECEIVE THE HOLY SPIRIT

We must confess our sins, acknowledging that Jesus is the only true way. We should acknowledge that God forgives us, and that the blood of Jesus cleanses us, making us righteous (in right standing with God). He saves us and adopts us as His children, giving us His Holy Spirit. We should have no other gods beside Him. The Spirit then instructs and empowers us to live a victorious Christian life.

HOW DID THE DISCIPLES RECEIVE THE HOLY SPIRIT?

In John 20:19-22, the disciples saw the risen savior and they were glad. They then believed that He was the risen Christ. He breathed on them, and they received the Holy Ghost. When any man acknowledges Jesus as the risen, living Son of God, and asks for forgiveness of sin, God will hear the sinner's cry. When a man is born again, he receives the Holy Spirit as a seal or earnest of his inheritance.

"²⁸After this I will pour out My Spirit on all humanity; then your sons and your daughters will prophesy, your old men will have dreams, and your young men will see visions. ²⁹I will even pour out My Spirit on the male and female slaves in those days." (Joel 2:28-29, HCSB)

What is the significance of this promise, and why did it make a difference? This promise of the latter-day outpouring of the Holy Spirit declared in Joel was fulfilled in Acts 2 on the day of Pentecost.

In the Old Testament, God spoke through prophets in dreams and visions. The Spirit would move upon prophets and give them a word for His people. He did not always permanently reside in prophets, kings, and priests. The Holy Spirit would come upon the people according to the need of the moment. The Spirit would anoint people to accomplish God's purpose for their lives, thereby impacting their generation. An example of this is seen in Zechariah 4:6, when Zechariah prophesied by the Spirit and Zerubbabel was empowered by the Spirit to rebuild the temple. The study of a few more instances will show how the Holy Spirit came upon people in the Old Testament.

AZARIAH

The Holy Spirit came upon Azariah and he received a prophetic word from God for His people. Asa heard the words, acted upon them, and brought about the desired change in the nation.

"So he went out to meet Asa and said to him, "Asa and all Judah and Benjamin, hear me. The Lord is with you when you are with Him. If you seek Him, He will be found by you, but if you abandon Him, He will abandon you." (2 Chron. 15:2, HCSB)

"When Asa heard these words and the prophecy of Azariah, son of Oded the prophet, he took courage and removed the detestable idols from the whole land of Judah and Benjamin and from the cities he had captured in the hill country of Ephraim. He renovated the altar of the Lord that was in front of the portico of the Lord's temple." (2 Chron. 15:8, HCSB)

"Then they entered into a covenant to seek the Lord God of their ancestors with all their mind and all their heart." (2 Chron. 15:12, HCSB)

EZEKIEL

> "As He spoke to me, the Spirit entered me and set me on my feet, and I listened to the One who was speaking to me." (Ezek. 2:2, HCSB)

The Spirit of the Lord came upon Ezekiel appointing him a prophet to the captives in Babylon.

SAMSON

In the book of Judges, the Jews would fall away from God, and they would be given into the hands of their enemies. The Jews would cry out to God, and He would send a judge to deliver them. Samson was one such judge. Even though Samson had major flaws, God empowered him to bring about deliverance to Israel.

> "Then the Spirit of the Lord began to direct him in the Camp of Dan, between Zorah and Eshtaol..." (Judg. 13:25, HCSB)

> "14When he came to Lehi, the Philistines came to meet him shouting. The Spirit of the Lord took control of him, and the ropes that were on his arms became like burnt flax and his bonds fell off his wrists. 15He found a fresh jawbone of a donkey, reached out his hand, took it, and killed 1,000 men with it." (Judg. 15:14-15, HCSB)

Here the Spirit came upon Samson, enabling him to do the impossible – single-handedly kill 1,000 men!

> "...But he did not know that the Lord had left him." (Judg. 16:20, HCSB)

Delilah sweet-talked Samson into divulging the secret of his superhuman strength, which was 'rooted' in his hair. A Nazarite's long hair was a sign of his consecration to God for a period of time. When the vow was fulfilled, the Nazarite would cut his hair. Samson was dedicated to be a Nazarite for life. After his capture, he prayed to receive supernatural strength through the Spirit. He killed more Philistines during his last stand than ever before.

SAUL

> "Samuel took the flask of oil, poured it out on Saul's head, kissed him, and said, "Hasn't the Lord anointed you ruler over His inheritance?" (1 Sam. 10:1, HCSB)

> "The Spirit of the Lord will control you, you will prophesy with them, and you will be transformed into a different person." (1 Sam. 10:6, HCSB)

> "Then the Spirit of God took control of him, and he prophesied along with them." (1 Sam. 10:10, HCSB)

Saul was chosen to be the king of Israel. He was anointed with oil, and the Holy Spirit came upon him, empowering him to be an effective king.

In 1 Samuel 15, God commands Saul to destroy Amalek completely. Everything that breathed was to be wiped out. Saul obeyed only in part as he left the best of the cattle and sheep to be sacrificed to the Lord. However, God wanted his complete obedience. Since Saul rejected the word of the Lord, God rejected him as king, and chose David instead.

> "Samuel replied to Saul, "I will not return with you. Because you rejected the word of the Lord, the Lord has rejected you from being king over Israel." (1 Sam. 15:26, HCSB)

> "Samuel said to him, "The Lord has torn the kingship of Israel away from you today and has given it to your neighbor who is better than you." (1 Sam. 15:28, HCSB)

After Saul was rejected, the Spirit left him.

> "Now the Spirit of the Lord had left Saul, and an evil spirit sent from the Lord began to torment him." (1 Sam.16:14, HCSB)

The Lord permitted this evil spirit to torment Saul as punishment for Saul's failure to yield himself to God. Most likely, evil spirits were trying to torment Saul from the moment that he surrendered his heart to jealousy over David's success. Once the Spirit of God left him, God's protection was removed, and the evil spirits were able to torment Saul.

DAVID

> "So Samuel took the horn of oil, anointed him in the presence of his brothers, and the Spirit of the Lord took control of David from that day forward..." (1 Sam. 16:13, HCSB)

The Holy Spirit came upon David, empowering him to drive out the giants from Canaan and be a good king to Israel. After David committed adultery, he repented and prayed, as depicted in Psalm 51:11 (HCSB), "Do not banish me from Your presence or take Your Holy Spirit from me." The reason for David's request was that he had seen up close how the Spirit had left Saul, and David did not want to experience a similar fate.

JOHN THE BAPTIST

> "...and he shall be filled with the Holy Ghost, while still in his mother's womb."
> (Luke 1:15, HCSB)

John was filled with the Holy Spirit because he was chosen to be the herald who would declare the way of the Lord. As a forerunner, John preached the coming of the Messiah, preparing people's hearts for the coming of the Lord. John went forth, a voice crying in the wilderness, in the same spirit and power of Elijah.

The sign by which John could identify who the Messiah would be was that the Spirit would descend on Him and remain on Him.

> "And I knew Him not: but he that sent me to baptize with water, the same said unto me, Upon whom thou shalt see the Spirit descending, and remaining on Him, the same is he which baptizeth with the Holy Ghost. [34] And I saw, and bare record that this is the Son of God." (John 1:33-34, KJV)

> "...and the Holy Spirit descended on Him in a physical appearance like a dove. And a voice came from heaven: You are My beloved Son. I take delight in You!" (Luke 3: 22, HCSB)

This occurrence was an unusual phenomenon because up to this point in history, the Holy Spirit generally came upon people only temporarily for a specific time and purpose. Previously, the Holy Spirit did not descend on just anyone. The Spirit remained on Jesus, marking the start of a new move of God.

In Acts, the Holy Spirit was poured out on ordinary, born-again people, and surprisingly, even the Gentiles. God desires to pour out His Spirit on all flesh. When Jesus spoke of the Holy Spirit, He said that the Holy Spirit will always remain with us. He will never leave us nor forsake us.

> "And I will ask the Father, and He will give you another Counselor to be with you forever." (John 14:16, HCSB)

PENTECOST: THE BAPTISM OF THE HOLY SPIRIT

"⁴While He was together with them, He commanded them not to leave Jerusalem, but to wait for the Father's promise. "This," He said, "is what you heard from Me. ⁵For John baptized with water, but you will be baptized with the Holy Spirit not many days from now." (Acts 1:4-5, HCSB)

Jesus gave the disciples these instructions before He ascended to heaven:

"But you will receive power when the Holy Spirit has come on you, and you will be My witnesses in Jerusalem, in all Judea and Samaria, and to the ends of the earth" (Acts 1:8, HCSB)

The disciples had already received the Holy Spirit in John 20:19-22. However, they still lacked power and boldness as they went fishing when they should have been preaching about the Christ. Jesus promised them that they would receive the power (*dunamis*) when the Holy Spirit came upon them. Without the power of the Holy Spirit operative in our life, we will struggle in our own might as we try to accomplish things for God. We cannot live a victorious Christian life on our own.

We all **receive** the Spirit when we are born again. We are like a container that holds some water, but when we are **baptized** in the Holy Spirit, our container is **immersed** in the water. We no longer just contain Him – He saturates our being and we are submerged in Him. Do you see the difference? This is such a glorious experience! Oh, that we would have more of Him!

The baptism in the Holy Spirit had a profound effect on the disciples. It empowered them to testify boldly of Jesus' death and resurrection. After this event, they travelled all over the world preaching about Jesus.

"When the day of Pentecost had arrived, they were all together in one place. ²Suddenly a sound like that of a violent rushing wind came from heaven, and it filled the whole house where they were staying. ³And tongues, like flames of fire that were divided, appeared to them and rested on each one of them. ⁴Then they were all filled with the Holy Spirit and began to speak in different languages, as the Spirit gave them ability for speech." (Acts 2: 1-4, HCSB)

Observe the kind of disciple that Peter was before he was baptized in the Holy Ghost. He boasted, making great proclamations about his devotion to Christ. Peter certainly had good intentions, but when the time came, he betrayed Jesus. He behaved according to the meaning of his other name *Simon* – a reed tossed by the wind. After he was baptized with the Holy Ghost, the same man walked into the destiny that Christ had for him. No longer ashamed of Christ, he became *Peter* – a rock. After this, he preached the gospel boldly, and 3,000 people were saved in one service.

Pentecost was one of the eight festivals of Jehovah. The word *Pentecost* originates from the Greek language and means 'fifty'. The Pentecostal feast falls 50 days after the festival of First Fruits.

The festivals of Israel are all 'shadows of the Messiah'. Of the eight Feasts, we will look at the four which are a spiritual parallel to the Death, Burial, Resurrection of Jesus, and the Outpouring of the Holy Spirit.

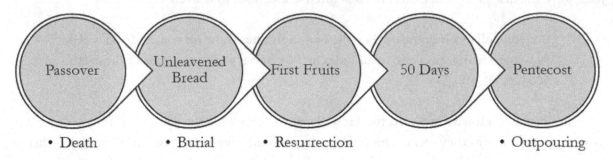

Passover	Unleavened Bread	First Fruits	50 Days	Pentecost
• Death	• Burial	• Resurrection		• Outpouring

Passover to Pentecost

Significance of the Festivals of Israel

PASSOVER			
Date of Festival	Historical aspect	Messianic prophecy	Spiritual Parallel
On the 14th of Nisan	An unblemished lamb was killed. Its blood was put on the doorpost of each house. The Angel of Death "passed over" such a house, and all the inhabitants were safe.	Death of Jesus	Christ is our sinless Passover lamb (1 Cor. 5:7) When we stay under the blood, the destroyer will not come near us.
UNLEAVENED BREAD			
Date of Festival	Historical aspect	Messianic prophecy	Spiritual Parallel
On the 15th of Nisan	The Israelites were commanded to make unleavened bread as they had to leave Egypt in haste. Unleavened bread was to be eaten for seven days. No leaven was to be found in homes.	Burial of Jesus	Shows that Jesus was the sinless one. Leaven = wickedness; Unleavened bread= sincerity and truth (1 Cor. 5:8)

FIRST FRUITS			
Date of Festival	Historical aspect	Messianic prophecy	Spiritual Parallel
On the third day after Passover	The wheat that ripened earliest was collected as a sheaf and presented as first fruits as a wave offering.	Resurrection of Jesus	Jesus is the first fruit of resurrection (1 Cor. 15:20-23)
PENTECOST			
Date of Festival	Historical aspect	Messianic prophecy	Spiritual Parallel
50 days from the festival of First Fruits	Seven Sabbaths were counted from the feast of First Fruits. On the 50th day, two leavened loaves were made from the first fruits of the wheat harvest and were offered as a wave offering.	Outpouring of the Holy Spirit. 50 days after the resurrection of Christ	Jesus is the One who baptizes with the Holy Spirit and fire (Luke 3:16).

Fifty days after Passover, the disciples were filled with the Holy Spirit in the upper room on the day of Pentecost. In Acts 2:16, Peter declared that this was the fulfillment of the promise in Joel 2:28 and 29.

> "28After this I will pour out My Spirit on all humanity; then your sons and your daughters will prophesy, your old men will have dreams, and your young men will see visions. 29I will even pour out My Spirit on the male and female slaves in those days." (Joel 2:28-29, HCSB)

Peter preached boldly about Christ and 3,000 people were added to the church. In Acts 2:37, (HCSB), they were convicted and asked, "Brothers, what shall we do"?

> "38Repent, Peter said to them, "and be baptized, each of you, in the name of Jesus Christ for the forgiveness of your sins, and you will receive the **gift** of the Holy Spirit. 39For the promise is for you and for your children, and for all who are far off as many as the Lord our God will call." (Acts 2:38-39, HCSB)

This is the promise of the New Covenant. The Holy Spirit will be given to all who repent and believe in the name of Jesus.

> "If you then, who are evil, know how to give good gifts to your children, how much more will the heavenly Father give the Holy Spirit to those who ask Him?" (Luke 11:13, HCSB)

This verse reveals to us the nature of God. The Father will not withhold the gift of the Spirit from His children. The purpose of the baptism of the Holy Spirit is to be empowered to witness about Jesus, to live a victorious Christian life, to reflect God's glory, and to be changed into His image by the Spirit.

SECTION 2
SYMBOLS OF THE HOLY SPIRIT

SYMBOLS OF THE HOLY SPIRIT

1. WIND

Wind is invisible. Though we cannot see it, we can feel the wind and see its effects.

BE BORN AGAIN

> "⁶Whatever is born of the flesh is flesh, and whatever is born of the Spirit is spirit. ⁷Do not be amazed that I told you that you must be born again. ⁸The wind blows where it pleases, and you hear its sound, but you don't know where it comes from or where it is going. So it is with everyone born of the Spirit." (John 3:6-8, HCSB)

Just as we have a physical birth, our spirit must be regenerated, or born again. This is a spiritual birth. This happens when the Spirit gives life to a dead human spirit. The Holy Spirit is like the wind, which can neither be controlled nor directed by us. The Spirit moves at God's direction, just like the wind. We cannot predict His next move.

In John 3:8, the word 'wind' is translated from the Greek word *pneuma* which means: 'Spirit' (The Holy Spirit or a human spirit) or 'Wind' (a gentle movement of air or a breath from the nostrils or mouth).

> "...The first man Adam became a living being; the last Adam became a life-giving Spirit. (1 Cor. 15:45, HCSB)

When God created Adam, He made his body of flesh and breathed His Spirit (*pneuma*) into him.

> "Then the Lord God formed the man out of the dust from the ground and breathed the breath of life into his nostrils, and the man became a living being." (Gen. 2:7, HCSB)

Adam died spiritually when he sinned and was separated from God. Adam begat the same sinful flesh.

> "Whatever is born of the flesh is flesh, and whatever is born of the Spirit is spirit." (John 3:6, HCSB)

Jesus came as the 'last Adam', a life-giving spirit. Our dead spirits can be made alive only because Jesus is alive. His Spirit gives birth to our spirit, and we are born again.

> "After saying this, He breathed on them and said, "Receive the Holy Spirit." (John 20:22, HCSB)

The Greek word for 'breathed' is used in the same context as that in Gen 2:7, when God created Adam. On the day of Jesus' resurrection, those who believed in the risen Christ were made a new creation. The disciples believed and received the Holy Spirit. We can receive the Holy Spirit once we believe in Jesus' name.

BE FILLED WITH THE HOLY GHOST

> "Suddenly a sound like that of a violent rushing wind came from heaven, and it filled the whole house where they were staying." (Acts 2:2, HCSB)

This is during the outpouring of the Holy Spirit on the early church, just after Jesus' resurrection. The believers were assembled in prayer in Jerusalem. Suddenly, the Holy Spirit came as a mighty, rushing wind, and the believers received the baptism of the Holy Ghost.

THE DEAD BECOME ALIVE

> "⁹He said to me, "Prophesy to the breath, prophesy, son of man. Say to it: This is what the Lord God says: Breath, come from the four winds and breathe into these slain so that they may live!" ¹⁰So I prophesied as He commanded me; the breath entered them, and they came to life and stood on their feet, a vast army. ¹¹Then He said to me, "Son of man, these bones are the whole house of Israel. Look how they say, 'Our bones are dried up, and our hope has perished; we are cut off.'" (Ezek. 37: 9-11, HCSB)

This is a message to God's exiled people in Babylon. The dried bones represented the house of Israel. They were stripped of country, king, priest, homes, and possessions. They were scattered and sold to serve in Babylon. Verse 11 shows us that the dried bones represent their hope that was cut off. They saw no way out of their situation. The Jewish nation was wiped out, their temple burnt to the ground, their Davidic line of kings was no longer ruling. They were like a branch that was cast off.

> "I will put My Spirit in you, and you will live, and I will settle you in your own land..." (Ezek. 37:14, HCSB)

God was promising to bring them out of their graves. The wind in this story represents the Holy Spirit bringing dead Israel back to life. When we allow the wind of the Holy Spirit to blow over our lives, He will bring decayed, withered areas to life.

2. WATER

> "He saved us – not by works of righteousness that we had done, but according to His mercy, through the washing of regeneration and renewal by the Holy Spirit." (Titus 3:5, HCSB)

The new birth is associated with washing by the Holy Spirit. In the physical realm, washing with water cleanses away dirt. Likewise, the Holy Spirit washes us as water does, cleansing us from the filth of sin when we are born again.

> "²⁵I will also sprinkle clean water on you, and you will be clean. I will cleanse you from all your impurities and all your idols. ²⁶I will give you a new heart and put a new spirit within you; I will remove your heart of stone and give you a heart of flesh." (Ezek. 36:25-26, HCSB)

When Jesus spoke to the woman at the well, He spoke of the Holy Spirit as living water. Just as the human body cannot live without water, so our spirits cannot live without the Holy Ghost. He is the water to the thirsty soul.

> "But whoever drinks from the water that I will give him will never get thirsty again – ever! In fact, the water I will give him will become a well of water springing up within him for eternal life." (John 4:14, HCSB)

> "³⁷…Jesus stood up and cried out, "If anyone is thirsty, he should come to Me and drink! ³⁸The one who believes in Me, as the Scripture has said, will have streams of living water flow from deep within him."" (John 7:37-38, HCSB)

3. OIL

In scripture, the anointing with oil and the Holy Ghost go hand in hand. Kings and priests were anointed with special anointing oil. This represented the Holy Spirit coming upon the individual, empowering him or her to fulfill God's will.

DAVID

> "So Samuel took the horn of oil, anointed him in the presence of his brothers, and the Spirit of the Lord took control of David from that day forward…." (1 Sam. 16:13, HCSB)

JESUS

Jesus was anointed with the oil of gladness. There is no record of this physically happening. This is referring to the spiritual anointing of Jesus.

> "You love righteousness and hate wickedness; therefore, God, your God, has anointed you with the oil of joy more than your companions." (Ps. 45:7, HCSB)

ZERUBBABEL

Zechariah 4 details Zechariah's vision of a golden candlestick with seven lamps. It was just like the candlestick in the Temple in Exodus 27:20-21. In the Temple, the priests had to keep filling the lamps with oil, day and night. In the vision, the lamps received a continuous supply of oil from the two olive trees beside it. Here, the oil represents the Holy Spirit. The message is that Zerubbabel was to complete the construction of the Temple against all odds, by the anointing and power of the Holy Spirit.

> "… Then he said to me, "This [continuous supply of oil] is the word of the Lord to Zerubbabel [prince of Judah], saying, 'Not by might, nor by power, but by My Spirit [of whom the oil is a symbol],' says the Lord of hosts." (Zech. 4:6, AMP)

Zechariah asked about the golden branches beside the golden tubes by which the oil was being emptied out. This is the answer given to Zechariah.

> "Then he said, "These are the two sons of fresh oil [Joshua the high priest and Zerubbabel the prince of Judah] who are standing by the Lord of the whole earth [as His anointed ones]." (Zech. 4:14, AMP)

Joshua and Zerubbabel were the two 'Sons of Oil' that God used to fulfill His purpose in their generation. The Temple would be rebuilt, not of their own might, but only because of the anointing of the Holy Spirit flowing through them. The anointing upon them enabled them to accomplish God's plan on the earth.

4. THE DOVE

> "And John testified, "I watched the Spirit descending from heaven like a dove, and He rested on Him." (John 1:32, HCSB)

PEACE

The dove is considered a symbol of peace. When Noah released the dove from the ark, the dove returned with an olive leaf in its beak. This was evidence that peace had returned to the earth, and that God's wrath and judgement had passed.

It is the Holy Spirit who draws unbelievers to God with the gospel of peace. Isaiah 61:1 talks about the Spirit being upon the Messiah to preach good tidings, bind up the brokenhearted, proclaim liberty, and proclaim the acceptable year of the Lord. He witnesses to our hearts that Jesus has brought peace through the blood of the cross, reconciling God and the sinner.

PURITY

The Spirit is pure, spotless, and holy. In Him there is nothing unclean or impure.

HUMILITY AND MEEKNESS

The Holy Spirit is a gentleman. He is never forceful or tyrannical. He imparts these characteristics to us as we allow His presence to increase in our lives.

HE CAN BE GRIEVED

A dove is easily frightened. Likewise, the Spirit can be grieved by our actions, words, and thoughts. We must be very sensitive to the Holy Spirit. We are warned in Ephesians 4:30 not to grieve God's Holy Spirit.

5. WELLS

> "But whoever drinks from the water that I will give him will never get thirsty again – ever! In fact, the water I will give him will become a well of water springing up within him for eternal life." (John 4:14, HCSB)

Jesus likens the Holy Ghost to a well of life. In the Old Testament, many people had spiritual experiences around wells. In Old Testament times, people couldn't survive in the wilderness for long without a water source. Usually, desert dwellers dug a well and settled around it.

HAGAR

> "The Angel of the Lord found her by a spring of water in the wilderness, the spring on the way to Shur." (Gen. 16:7, HCSB)

Hagar received a command, a direction, a blessing, and a prophecy.

> "So she called the Lord who spoke to her: The God Who Sees, for she said, "In this place, have I actually seen the One who sees me?" (Gen. 16:13, HCSB)

She called the name of the Lord who spoke to her *El Roi*, which means 'The Living One who sees me.' She had an encounter with God that changed her life and caused her to walk in the blessing of God.

> "That is why she named the spring, "A Well of the Living One Who Sees Me."" (Gen. 16:14, HCSB)

The well was named *Beer-lahai-roi*. The word *Beer* means 'well.' The naming of the well *Beer-lahai-roi* meant 'The well of the Living One who sees me.' Without the leading of the Holy Spirit, we are like Hagar running away from God's plan for our life. In the wilderness of life, the Holy Spirit gives us direction and instruction, so we can walk in God's blessings. In Gen 21:16-20, we see how Hagar ran out of water in the wilderness. When Ishmael cried out, God heard him and showed Hagar a well. They drank and lived.

ABRAHAM AND ISAAC

"²⁵But Abraham complained to Abimelech because of the water well that Abimelech's servants had seized. ²⁶Abimelech replied, "I don't know who did this thing. You didn't report anything to me, so I hadn't heard about it until today." ²⁷Abraham took sheep and cattle and gave them to Abimelech, and the two of them made a covenant. ²⁸Abraham separated seven ewe lambs from the flock. ²⁹And Abimelech said to Abraham, "Why have you separated these seven ewe lambs?" ³⁰He replied, "You are to accept the seven ewe lambs from my hand so that this act will serve as my witness that I dug this well." ³¹Therefore that place was called Beer-sheba because it was there that the two of them swore an oath." (Gen. 21:25-31, HCSB)

The Philistines fought for the wells that Abraham dug. They filled up his wells with dirt. This happened in Isaac's time as well. The devil will fight to take away the wells of experience that we have with the Holy Ghost. Whenever we dig a well, he wants to fill it up with dirt. The devil knows that we can walk in the abundant life that God has for us when we dig deep into our hearts and allow the Holy Spirit to spring up inside of us.

"Now Isaac was returning from *Beer-lahai-roi*, for he was living in the Negev region."
(Gen. 24:62, HCSB)

Isaac is seen living at the *Beer-lahai-roi* (the well of the Living One who sees me) at the time of his wedding to Rebekah.

"¹⁵The Philistines stopped up all the wells that his father's slaves had dug in the days of his father Abraham, filling them with dirt. ¹⁶And Abimelech said to Isaac, "Leave us, for you are much too powerful for us." ¹⁷So Isaac left there, camped in the Valley of Gerar, and lived there. ¹⁸Isaac reopened the water wells that had been dug in the days of his father Abraham and that the Philistines had stopped up after Abraham died. He gave them the same names his father had given them." (Gen. 26:15-18, HCSB)

In verse 17, Isaac pitched his tent in Gerar. Like Isaac dug the wells, God wants us to dig up the 'fallow ground' of our hearts, and make way for the life-spring of the Holy Ghost.

(A) ESEK (QUARREL / CONTENTION)

> "¹⁹Then Isaac's slaves dug in the valley and found a well of spring water there. ²⁰But the herdsmen of Gerar quarreled with Isaac's herdsmen and said, "The water is ours!" So he named the well Quarrel because they quarreled with him." (Gen. 26:19-20, HCSB)

The Philistines fought with Isaac over three wells. The enemy will put up a fight every time we attempt to dig deeper into the realm of the Holy Ghost, and he is clearly intimidated by believers who walk in the power of the Holy Spirit. Isaac named the well *Esek* or 'Quarrel'. He did not let the contention slow him down or prevent his progress. Like Isaac, we must move forward and keep digging, despite the opposition.

(B) SITNAH (ENMITY / STRIFE)

> "Then they dug another well and quarreled over that one also, so he named it Hostility." (Gen. 26:21, HCSB)

The enemy continued to put up a fight over another well, given the name *Sitnah* or 'Hostility'. Isaac, however, was not deterred. He did not give up or lose heart. Does it seem like we experience the same problems? Does it feel as though certain people trouble us all the time? The blessing of God will be upon us as we continue to seek (dig) after Him. God will put all our enemies to flight as He brings us into the spacious place.

> "When a man's ways please the Lord, He makes even his enemies to be at peace with him." (Pro. 16:7, HCSB).

(C) REHEBOTH (SPACIOUSNESS / WIDE PLACES)

> "He moved from there and dug another, and they did not quarrel over it. He named it Open Spaces, and said, "For now the Lord has made room for us, and we will be fruitful in the land."" (Gen. 26:22, HCSB)

The third well was named *Rehoboth,* or 'Open Spaces'. The Lord is able to make "room for us" so that we may bear fruit for Him. Our job is to keep on digging.

(D) BEERSHEBA (THE WELL OF THE OATH / SEVEN)

This was the well at which Abraham made an oath with Abimelech. In Isaac's time, the enemy approached Isaac and made him promise them that he would do them no harm.

> "²⁸ They replied, "We have clearly seen how the Lord has been with you. We think there should be an oath between two parties — between us and you. Let us make

a covenant with you: ²⁹ You will not harm us, just as we have not harmed you but have only done what was good to you, sending you away in peace. You are now blessed by the Lord." (Gen. 26:28-29, HCSB)

As Isaac progressed from one well to another, he grew in might. It is plain to see that God was his defense. The Philistines were not just intimidated by his power and influence; they were terrified of Isaac. They made an oath with him for their own safety. It was as though they were begging him not to hurt them. As we advance from glory to glory, the enemy will get intimidated by our belief and be afraid for his own safety, because it is clear that 'God is with us'.

6. RAIN

"May he be like rain that falls on the cut grass, like spring showers that water the earth." (Ps. 72: 6, HCSB)

We understand the importance of rain to the land. Rain comes down upon the earth and the land bears fruit. In drought, all vegetation and animal life begin to die. Farmers expect rain twice in the growing season. The early and latter rain is mentioned throughout scripture. The early rains of autumn cause seeds to sprout. In the springtime, the rain falls again, giving new life. After this latter rain, the crops grow rapidly until harvest. The early rain is like the initial outpouring on the early church in the book of Acts. Now we are in the time of the latter rain, when the church needs to be revived before the coming of Christ, which is the harvest.

The first instance of the early and latter rain is in Deuteronomy.

"¹³If you carefully obey my commands I am giving you today, to love the Lord your God and worship Him with all your heart and all your soul, ¹⁴I will provide rain for your land in the proper time, the autumn and spring rains, and you will harvest your grain, new wine, and oil." (Deut. 11:13-14, HCSB)

The Israelites in Jeremiah's time were rebellious and unrepentant. They did not realize that the source of life-giving rain was the Lord from whom they had departed.

"This is why the showers haven't come – why there has been no spring rain..." (Jer. 3:3, HCSB)

Idolatry in Israel caused the blessing of rain to be withheld.

"They have not said to themselves, 'Let's fear the Lord our God, who gives the rain, both early and late, in its season, who guarantees to us the fixed weeks of the harvest.'" (Jer. 5:24, HCSB)

In Hosea 6, the prophet calls fickle Israel to return to God. If they obeyed, God would draw near to them. He would come to them as the refreshing rain.

> "Let us strive to know the Lord. His appearance is as sure as the dawn. He will come
> to us like the rain, like the spring showers that water the land." (Hos. 6:3, HCSB)

In Joel 2, the priests were called to weep between the porch and the altar. Israel was called to turn to God and rend its hearts before Him. God would then do great things, as evidenced in verses 21 and 22.

> "Children of Zion, rejoice and be glad in the Lord your God, because He gives you
> the autumn of rain for your vindication. He sends showers for you, both autumn
> and spring rain as before." (Joel 2:23, HCSB)

We need to ask God for the rain of the Holy Ghost, otherwise we will 'dry up' like parched land.

> "Ask the Lord for rain in the season of spring rain. The Lord makes the rain clouds,
> and He will give them showers of rain and crops in the field for everyone." (Zech.
> 10:1, HCSB)

7. FIRE

The Holy Spirit is depicted as a holy fire.

> "The appearance of the Lord's glory to the Israelites was like a consuming fire on
> the mountaintop." (Ex. 24:17, HCSB)

Throughout scripture, God's presence was accompanied by fire. There is a multitude of examples of the Lord appearing in a fire: Moses saw the burning bush (Ex. 3:2-4); God went before the Israelites as a fire by night (Ex. 13:21, HCSB); When Israel received the Ten Commandments, God spoke to them out of the midst of the fire (Deut. 5:23-26, HCSB); Elijah's sacrifice was burned up by the fire of the Lord (1 Kings 18:38, HCSB).

> "²But who can endure the day of His coming? And who will be able to stand when
> He appears? For He will be like a refiner's fire and like cleansing lye. ³He will be
> like a refiner and purifier of silver; He will purify the sons of Levi and refine them
> like gold and silver. Then they will present offerings to the Lord in righteousness."
> (Mal. 3:2-3, HCSB)

The fire of His presence refines us and removes all impurity. At the same time, the fire of His presence is awesome and glorious.

In Matthew 3:11(HCSB), John the Baptist spoke of Jesus, saying, "...He Himself will baptize you with the Holy Spirit and fire". When the disciples received the baptism of the Holy Ghost, the Spirit was seen descending on them as cloven tongues of fire.

> "And tongues, like flames of fire that were divided, appeared to them and rested on each one of them." (Acts 2:3, HCSB)

We need the fire of the Holy Ghost. It gives us supernatural zeal to do His will. The fire gives us awe and reverence for God. The refiner's fire cleanses us from everything unholy.

> "... For our God is a consuming fire." (Heb. 12:29, HCSB)

8. SEAL AND EARNEST

> "He has also sealed us and given us the Spirit as a down payment in our hearts." (2 Cor. 1:22, HCSB)

The word 'earnest' as used in KJV can be understood as a down payment or guarantee. The Spirit is a seal on our hearts, signifying that we are bought and paid for, and that we belong to God. The Spirit reminds us that we belong to God, and that He is coming back for us.

> "13When you heard the message of truth, the gospel of your salvation, and when you believed in Him, you were also sealed with the promised Holy Spirit. 14 He is the down payment of our inheritance, for the redemption of the possession, to the praise of His glory." (Eph. 1:13-14, HCSB)

Redemption happens in two stages. In the first stage, the blood of Christ secures our salvation, position, and title. Only at the second stage will the actual possession be ours. We are familiar with transactions made up of two phases. For example, consider the first phase of purchasing a home. The buyer and the seller sign a contract agreeing to finalize the 'closing' of the house at a stated future date. A token amount referred to as 'earnest money' is paid by the buyer, showing the buyer's intent to complete the transaction on a set date in the future.

In ancient times, during the first phase of buying a plot of land during which the down payment was made, the seller would give the buyer a small sack with dirt from the property as a symbol of their agreement. It was a promise made to follow through until the transaction was complete, and that neither party would back out of the agreement. On a later day during the second stage of the transaction, the buyer would pay the promised amount, and the seller would hand over the title of ownership of the property.

We are in-between these two phases of redemption. Jesus has redeemed our spirits from death, but our bodies await the final redemption. In 2 Corinthians 5:1-5, Paul talks about our earthly bodies which will be transformed into a glorious body. Our body is but a temporary dwelling (like a tent) for our spirit, and its mortality will be engulfed by life as we are completely transformed to become like Him. In 1 Corinthians 15: 35-54, Paul talks about different bodies having differing glories. Just as terrestrial bodies differ from celestial bodies, so also does the human body differ from the glorified body of the redeemed believer. Adam was created out of dust, a natural man. Jesus was resurrected in a glorified body, a spiritual man. We too will follow this progression. We are born like Adam (a natural man) but will go through metamorphosis at rapture, in the 'twinkling of an eye'.

We will then have a glorified body like Christ.

> "And the One who prepared us for this very purpose is God, who gave us the Spirit as a down payment..." (2 Cor. 5:5, HCSB)

Chapter 5 of 2 Corinthians describes us as being clothed with a heavenly body. This will replace our mortal body. The seal of the Holy Spirit is the guarantee that this will come to pass.

Romans 8:22-23 states that even all creation has been groaning for this redemption to happen, because this fallen earth knows that its redemption is linked to the final redemption of the sons of God. After we receive our glorified bodies, the Earth will be renewed by fire, and the shackles of Adam's curse will fall.

SECTION 3
SPIRIT OF LIFE, WISDOM, AND REVELATION

SPIRIT OF LIFE

We cannot survive without water. Today we can take it for granted, but in biblical times water was treasured.

> "³⁷…If anyone is thirsty, he should come to Me and drink! ³⁸ The one who believes in Me, as the Scripture has said, will have streams of living water flow from deep within him." (John 7:37-38, HCSB)

We thirst, so we come to Jesus and drink. When we believe, our thirst is quenched from the river of the Holy Ghost which flows out of our belly or innermost being!

John 4:6-14 talks about how Jesus enters Samaria and sits by Jacob's well. Jesus is the Well or Fountain of Living Waters. Essentially, the 'Spiritual Well' Himself sat beside a physical well.

> "But whoever drinks from the water that I will give him will never get thirsty again – ever! In fact, the water I will give him will become a well of water springing up within him for eternal life." (John 4:14, HCSB)

The word *paga* means a fountain, spring, or a well fed by a spring. This represented a source of life, especially for travelers in the desert. People always dug wells and camped about them. When Israel needed water in the wilderness, God said that He would provide water.

> "Then Israel sang this song: Spring up, well – sing to it!" (Num. 21:17, HCSB)

GOD IS THE FOUNTAIN OF LIVING WATERS

> "For My people have committed a double evil: They have abandoned Me, the fountain of living water, and dug cisterns for themselves, cracked cisterns that cannot hold water." (Jer. 2:13, HCSB)

God is supposed to be the source of our life. Our lives are meant to be built and focused on Him. God's people forsook Him as their primary life spring and centered their lives around other things. In the absence of a well, cisterns were used to store rain water. People would run to these cisterns expecting to find fresh water, only to find that they were broken and holding stagnant water. These 'broken cisterns' are symbolic of anything or anybody we put our heart and soul into over experiencing the presence of God. If we run to these distractors in a time of trouble, we will find that they are broken and do not hold the healing waters of Life.

> "Lord, the hope of Israel, all who abandon You will be put to shame. All who turn away from Me will be written in the dirt, for they have abandoned the Lord, the fountain of living water." (Jer. 17:13, HCSB)

"⁷The man who trusts in the Lord, whose confidence indeed is the Lord, is blessed. ⁸He will be like a tree planted by water: it sends its roots out toward a stream, it doesn't fear when heat comes, and its foliage remains green. It will not worry in a year of drought or cease producing fruit." (Jer. 17:7-8, HCSB)

This is similar to Psalm 1:1-3, for the man whose delight is in the law of the Lord. We must be rooted in God's word and delight in it.

RIVER FLOWING OUT OF THE TEMPLE OF GOD

"Then he brought me back to the entrance of the temple and there was water flowing from under the threshold of the temple toward the east, for the temple faced east..." (Ezek. 47:1, HCSB)

The river increases in depth every 1,000 cubits. The water levels rise from being ankle deep, to knee-high, to waist deep, until it becomes 'a river that cannot be passed over'.

"⁷When I had returned; I saw a very large number of trees along both sides of the river bank. ⁸ He said to me, "This water flows out to the eastern region and goes down to the Arabah. When it enters the sea, the sea of foul water, the water of the sea becomes fresh. ⁹ Every kind of living creature that swarms will live wherever the river flows, and there will be a huge number of fish because this water goes there. Since the water will become fresh, there will be life everywhere the river goes." (Ezek. 47:7-9, HCSB)

This passage describes the river of life of the Holy Spirit bringing life and healing wherever it goes. The Holy Spirit makes dead things come to life. The fish represent people who will come to life and healing as the river engulfs them. Remember Jesus called us fishers of men.

"All kinds of trees providing food will grow along both banks of the river. Their leaves will not wither, and their fruit will not fail. Each month they will bear fresh fruit because the water comes from the sanctuary. Their fruit will be used for food and their leaves for medicine." (Ezek. 47:12, HCSB)

If we are like these trees, whose roots go down to the river of the Holy Ghost, we will bear spiritual fruit for God. We will fulfill God's purpose for our lives and bring food and healing to the dead people around us. Just as the waters come out of the sanctuary, the source of our Life should be from the presence of the Lord.

"Then he showed me the river of living water, sparkling like crystal, flowing from the throne of God and of the Lamb ²down the middle of the broad street of the city. The tree of life was on both sides of the river, bearing 12 kinds of fruit, producing its fruit every month. The leaves of the tree are for healing the nations, ³and there will no longer be any curse. The throne of God and of the Lamb will be in the city, and His slaves will serve Him." (Rev. 22:1-3, HCSB)

Compare this passage with the following passage from Genesis 2.

"⁸The Lord God planted a garden in Eden, in the east, and there He placed the man He had formed. ⁹The Lord God caused to grow out of the ground every tree pleasing in appearance and good for food, including the tree of life in the middle of the garden, as well as the tree of the knowledge of good and evil. ¹⁰A river went out from Eden to water the garden. From there it divided and became the source of four rivers." (Gen. 2:8-10, HCSB)

We see the same pattern running through scripture. The pattern in the book of Revelation is very similar to that of God's original creation in Eden.

God's will for our life is that we thirst and drink from Him by drawing Life from His Presence. Our innermost being will be a conduit for streams of living water. We will be as trees planted by this river, whose roots will go down to the river; whose leaves will not wither, and will bring healing; who will bear fruit for food, in season. If we allow this river to continually flow through us, we will be used to bring life and healing to the dead and needy around us.

SPIRIT OF WISDOM

"I pray that the God of our Lord Jesus Christ, the glorious Father would give you a Spirit of wisdom and revelation in the knowledge of Him." (Eph. 1:17, HCSB)

Have you ever wondered who Wisdom is? Who is this elusive person whom the scripture personifies as a woman?

THE SPIRIT OF WISDOM IS A PERSON

"God has united you with Christ Jesus. For our benefit God made Him to be wisdom itself." (1 Cor.1:30, KJV)

"...Christ is the power of God and the wisdom of God." (1 Cor. 1:24, NLT)

THE SPIRIT OF WISDOM IS THE SPIRIT OF THE LORD

"...and the Spirit of the Lord shall rest upon Him, the Spirit of wisdom and understanding...." (Isa. 11:2, HCSB)

THE SPIRIT OF WISDOM EXISTED BEFORE CREATION

"I was set up from everlasting, from the beginning, or ever the earth was." (Pro. 8:23, KJV)

"Before the mountains were brought forth, or ever thou hadst formed the earth and the world, even from everlasting to everlasting, thou art God." (Ps. 90:2, KJV)

"⁶Howbeit we speak wisdom among them...not the wisdom of this world, nor of the princes of this world... ⁷But we speak the wisdom of God in a mystery, even the hidden wisdom, which God ordained before the world unto our glory." (1 Cor. 2:6-7, KJV)

THE SPIRIT OF WISDOM WAS ACTIVE IN CREATING THE EARTH

"The Lord founded the earth by wisdom and established the heavens by understanding." (Pro. 3:19, HCSB)

God the Father, the Son, and the Holy Spirit were present at creation. As God created the world in the beginning, the Spirit of God was present with Him.

"In the beginning God created the heaven and the earth...the Spirit of God was hovering over the surfaces of the waters." (Gen. 1:1-2, HCSB)

In this passage, we see Wisdom beside God at creation.

THE SPIRIT OF WISDOM IS GOD

"Before the mountains were born, before You gave birth to the earth and the world, from eternity to eternity, You are God." (Ps. 90:2, HCSB)

"²⁴When there was no depths, I was brought forth; when there was no fountains abounding with water. ²⁵Before the mountains were settled, before the hills was I brought forth. ²⁶While as yet he had not made the earth or the fields, nor the highest part of the dust of the world. ²⁷When he prepared the heavens I was there: when he sat a compass upon the face of the depth: ²⁸When he established the clouds above: when he strengthened the fountains of the deep: ²⁹ When he gave to the sea His decree, that the waters should not pass His commandment: when he appointed the foundations of the earth: ³⁰Then I was by Him, as one brought up with Him: and I was daily His delight, rejoicing always before Him:" (Pro. 8:24-30, KJV)

Wisdom has been here from everlasting. The Spirit of Wisdom can be none other than the Spirit of the Lord.

"The Spirit of the Lord will rest on Him - a Spirit of wisdom and understanding, a Spirit of counsel and strength, a Spirit of knowledge and of the fear of the Lord." (Isa. 11:2, KJV)

THE SPIRIT OF WISDOM IS MANIFOLD

"To the intent that now unto the principalities and powers in heavenly places might be known by the church the manifold wisdom of God." (Eph. 3:10, KJV)

'Manifold' means a rich variety, multiple means of expression, and numerous traits. It should be no surprise that this is so.

"O the depths of the riches both of the wisdom and knowledge of God!" (Rom. 11:33a, KJV)

THE SPIRIT OF WISDOM IS BUT ONE OF SEVEN TRAITS OF GOD

In most Bible translations, the Book of Revelation refers to the Holy Spirit as 'the One Who has the seven spirits'. This could lead one to believe God has seven individual spirits!

> "...Grace be unto you, and peace, from Him which is, and which was, and which is to come; and from the seven Spirits which are before His throne." (Rev. 1:4, KJV)

But we know that the Holy Spirit is one spirit. As it is in Ephesians 4:4, "there is one body, and one Spirit..."and in Ephesians 2:18 "for through Him we both have access by one Spirit unto the Father."

THE SEVENFOLD SPIRIT

The New Living Translation (NLT) gives a more accurate definition of the word 'sevenfold'.

> "This is the message from the one who has the sevenfold Spirit of God..." (Rev. 3:1, NLT)

A tri-fold has three panels to it, yet it is three parts of a single board or paper. Likewise, the Holy Spirit is one spirit, but He has seven facets of His personality. These seven attributes are seen in Isaiah 11:2, as it mentions the Holy Spirit resting upon Jesus.

> "The Spirit of the Lord will rest on Him – a Spirit of wisdom and understanding, a Spirit of counsel and strength, a Spirit of knowledge and of the fear of the Lord." (Isa. 11:2, HCSB)

Seven is the number of perfection and completeness. The Holy Spirit has a sevenfold personality that can be characterized as the Spirit of the **Lord**; Spirit of **Wisdom**; Spirit of **Understanding**; Spirit of **Counsel**; Spirit of **Strength**; Spirit of **Knowledge**; and the Spirit of the **Fear of the Lord**.

The Spirit of Wisdom possesses the same seven characteristics that the Holy Spirit possesses. Or, put in another perspective, The Holy Spirit possesses the same seven qualities as the Spirit of Wisdom, which are beautifully described in Proverbs 8.

> "¹²I **wisdom** dwell with prudence, and find out **knowledge** of witty inventions. ¹³The **fear of the Lord** is to hate evil: pride, and arrogancy, and the evil way, and the froward mouth, do I hate. ¹⁴**Counsel** is mine, and sound wisdom: I am **understanding**; I have **strength**." (Pro. 8:12-14, KJV)

> "I was set up from **everlasting**, from the beginning, or ever the earth was." (Pro. 8:23, KJV)

We will look at each trait from Isaiah 11:2 that correspond to the seven traits seen in Wisdom of Proverbs 8.

1. SPIRIT OF THE LORD

The Holy Spirit is God, the Third Person of the Trinity. As we have seen in multiple instances in the Bible (Pro 8:23-30, Ps 90:2, Gen 1:2, Pro 3:19), He has always existed and created the world with the Father and the Son.

2. THE SPIRIT OF WISDOM

> "²⁰**Wisdom** calls out in the street; she raises her voice in the public squares. ²¹She cries out above the commotion; she speaks at the entrance of the city gates: ²²"How long, foolish ones, will you love ignorance? How long will you mockers enjoy mocking and you fools hate knowledge? ²³If you respond to my warning, then I will pour out my spirit on you and teach you my words." (Pro. 1:20-23, HCSB)

Wisdom calls us to leave the ways of foolishness. Each person has a choice to follow the call of Wisdom or to do their own thing. Without the wisdom of God, we are all fools. We may be intelligent and successful or possess human wisdom, but by Biblical standards we are foolish. If we respond to the reproof of wisdom and turn from our foolish ways, we can receive the Spirit, and He will make known His words to us, which are Truth and Life! Those who despise the call of wisdom and continue in their foolish ways will bear the consequences. As Proverbs 1:31 states, they will eat the fruit of their way and be glutted with their own schemes.

> "²⁸ Then shall they call upon me, but I will not answer; they shall seek me early, but they shall not find me: ²⁹For they hated knowledge and did not choose the fear of the Lord." (Pro. 1:28-29, KJV)

They will experience Proverbs 1:28 in contrast to those who seek after God and His wisdom.

> "I love them that love me, and those who seek me early shall find me." (Pro. 8:17, KJV)

3. THE SPIRIT OF UNDERSTANDING

> "Doesn't Wisdom call out? Doesn't **Understanding** make her voice heard?" (Pro. 8:1, HCSB)

Understanding is defined in Proverbs 9:10 (KJV), "The fear of the Lord is the beginning of wisdom, and the knowledge of the Holy One is understanding." The word 'understanding' means 'to have insight, intelligence, and skill'.

> "For the Lord gives wisdom; from His mouth come knowledge and understanding." (Pro. 2:6, HCSB)

Bezalel

God filled Bezalel with the Spirit of God so that he could make all the furniture in the Tabernacle.

> "² Look, I have appointed by name Bezalel son of Uri, son of Hur, of the tribe of Judah. ³I have filled him with God's Spirit, with wisdom, **understanding**, and ability in every craft." (Ex. 31:2-3, HCSB)

> "Bezalel, Oholiab, and all the skilled people are to work based on everything the Lord has commanded. The Lord has given them wisdom and **understanding** to know how to do all the work of constructing the sanctuary." (Ex. 36:1, HCSB)

Bezalel received wisdom from God. He was given the understanding required to create the articles of the Tabernacle according to God's design.

Understanding will also help us flee from evil. Once we receive the knowledge and understanding of God in our hearts, we will turn away from our own sinful ways and turn toward God.

> "...The fear of the Lord is this: wisdom. And to turn from evil is **understanding**." (Job 28:28, HCSB)

4. SPIRIT OF COUNSEL

> "**Counsel** is mine, and sound wisdom I have understanding and strength." (Pro. 8:14, KJV)

The Holy Spirit is our Counselor. Jesus said in John 14:16 (HCSB), "I will ask the Father, and He will give you another Counselor to be with you forever."

The word Counselor is taken from the Greek word *parakletos,* which means 'summoned' (called to one's side or aid); one who pleads another's cause before a judge, a pleader, counsel for defense, legal assistant, an advocate; or in the widest sense, a helper, succorer, aider, or assistant. The Holy Spirit is our advocate, helper, comforter, and counselor. In our time of need, He will come alongside us and help us like no one else can. When the Holy Spirit is allowed to work in our lives, He begins to impart these qualities into our lives.

The more of ourselves that we give to Him, the more He will increase and we will decrease. God will be able to fulfill His will in and through us more effectively.

5. SPIRIT OF STRENGTH (MIGHT)

> "...I have understanding and **strength**." (Pro. 8:14, HCSB)

The Holy Spirit has supernatural power that is beyond our comprehension. It is by this power that Christ was raised from the dead. The Holy Spirit empowers His people to accomplish His purpose as described in the verse below.

> "[19] ...and what is the exceeding greatness of His power toward us who believe, according to the working of His mighty power [20] which He worked in Christ when He raised Him from the dead and seated Him at His right hand in the heavenly places" (Eph. 1:19-20, KJV)

Samson

Samson is an example of superhuman strength because the Spirit of the Lord came upon him.

> "[14] ...The Spirit of the Lord took control of him, and the ropes that were on his arms became like burnt flax and his bonds fell off his wrists. [15] He found a fresh jawbone of a donkey, reached out his hand, took it, and killed 1,000 men with it." (Judg. 15:14-15, HCSB)

6. SPIRIT OF KNOWLEDGE

> "I wisdom dwell with prudence, and find out **knowledge** of witty inventions." (Pro. 8:12, KJV)

The knowledge that God gives is supernatural and surpasses the ordinary capabilities of man.

Daniel

Daniel and his friends were given supernatural wisdom, which enabled them to outshine all those around them.

> "God gave these four young men knowledge and understanding in every kind of literature and wisdom..." (Dan. 1:17, HCSB)

> "In every matter of wisdom and understanding that the king consulted them about, he found them 10 times better than all the diviner-priests and mediums in his entire kingdom." (Dan. 1:20, HCSB)

Solomon

When Solomon was faced with overwhelming task of governing Israel, he humbly sought God for wisdom.

> "[10]Now grant me wisdom and knowledge so that I may lead these people, for who can judge this great people of Yours?" [11]God said to Solomon, "Since this was in your heart, and you have not requested riches, wealth, or glory, or for the life of those who hate you, and you have not even requested long life, but you have requested for yourself wisdom and knowledge that you may judge My people over whom I have made you king, [12] wisdom and knowledge are given to you. I will also give you riches, wealth, and glory, unlike what was given to the kings who were before you, or will be given to those after you." (2 Chron. 1:10-12, HCSB)

God answered Solomon's prayer, and he became one of the wisest men in the world. Even when he was quizzed by the Queen of Sheba, he passed with flying colors, just as Daniel had succeeded before Nebuchadnezzar.

> "Solomon answered all her questions; nothing was too hard for him to explain to her." (2 Chron. 9:2, NIV)

7. SPIRIT OF THE FEAR OF THE LORD

> "To **fear the Lord** is to hate evil…" (Pro. 8:13, HCSB)

The word 'fear' here implies an awe and reverence for the Lord. This is a holy fear. If we truly fear and revere the Lord, we will hate evil and depart from all evil.

> "The fear of the Lord is a fountain of life, turning people away from the snares of death." (Pro. 14:27, HCSB)

> "The fear of the Lord is the beginning of wisdom…" (Pro. 9:10, KJV)

> "He said to mankind, "The fear of the Lord is this: wisdom. And to turn from evil is understanding." (Job 28:28, HCSB)

It is true that God is awesome and terrible and to be feared. The fear of the Lord has a more positive quality and is not to be equated with terror. I understand it as a fear of displeasing Him. It is also the fear of the distance that sin can bring between Him and us. This is a healthy fear that compels us to flee from sin and cleave to Him. It is not the same as the fear of a slave to his master, but of a child not wanting sin to destroy communion between a beloved parent and him. Joseph feared God. He did not commit adultery with Potiphar's wife because he knew it would be a great evil and sin against God. He realized that any sin committed against God would create a rift in his relationship with God.

SPIRIT OF REVELATION

"Where there is no revelation, the people cast off restraint; but happy is he who keeps the law." (Pro. 29:18, NKJV)

The Hebrew word for revelation is *chazown*, which means 'oracle, prophecy; communication (generally, a divine revelation); or a prophetic vision'.

"The revelation of Your words brings light and gives understanding to the inexperienced." (Ps. 119:130, HCSB)

The entrance or unveiling of God's word can be likened to unwrapping a gift. We are not able to see what is inside unless the wrapping is removed.

"It is the glory of God to conceal a matter and the glory of kings to investigate a matter." (Pro. 25:2, HCSB)

God keeps certain things secret. These are the mysteries in the Bible. These secrets need not remain locked forever. We will understand them only when God reveals them to us by His Spirit. We are the kings who have been bestowed with the honor to seek out the mysteries and secrets in God's word.

"For the froward *is* abomination to the Lord: but His secret is with the righteous" (Pro. 3:32, KJV)

The word 'secret' implies a council of familiar conversation (a divan, a circle of familiar friends, an assembly, a company) or a counsel (a secret counsel, familiar converse, an intimacy with God). God desires for us to know His secrets. In this context, the word *divan* refers to a couch, prop, or cushion. A *divan* was a long seat formed of a mattress laid upon the floor against the side of the room, or upon a raised structure or frame with cushions to lean against. A *divan* is an eastern council or a legislative body. The seat received its name because it was generally found along the walls in Middle Eastern council chambers of a bureau called *divan*. God desires to sit in intimate council with us, and reveal hidden counsel about Himself.

"Without revelation people run wild, but one who listens to instruction will be happy." (Pro. 29:18, HCSB)

The phrase 'run wild' comes from the Hebrew word *para*, which means 'being let loose, being loosened of restraint, to make unbridled, or lawless'. If we do not have a revelation of the Word and lack prophetic vision, we are in danger of becoming lawless. This is why some believers act like unbelievers. If we read the Word daily but lack revelation, we are not allowing the Spirit to transform and conform our lives and behavior to His image. An example of this is seen in Exodus.

The people of Israel were redeemed by the blood of the lamb from Egypt and were baptized into Moses in the Red Sea.

> "Now I want you to know, brothers, that our fathers were all under the cloud, all passed through the sea, ² and all were baptized into Moses in the cloud and in the sea." (1 Cor. 10:1-2, HCSB).

At Sinai, they made a golden calf and worshipped it.

> "...They arose, offered burnt offerings, and presented fellowship offerings. The people sat down to eat and drink, then got up to play. "(Ex. 32:6, HCSB)

The people of God were acting like pagans. It seemed as though they had never encountered God at all.

> "Now when Moses saw that the people were unrestrained (for Aaron had not restrained them, to their shame among their enemies) ..." (Ex. 32:25, NKJV)

As God's high priest, Aaron had the power and authority to control the crowd and prevent them from acting the way they did. When Aaron did not restrain them, the crowd went wild. Similarly, the Word has the power to keep us from ungodly behavior and sin. However, if we do not allow the Holy Spirit to give us the *rhema* word (illuminating of a scripture) necessary to transform our lives, we are in danger of becoming like the unrestrained Israelites.

> "The hidden things belong to the Lord our God, but the revealed things belong to us and our children forever, so that we may follow all the words of this law." (Deut. 29:29, HCSB)

When we receive the revelations of God's secrets and mysteries, it enables us to carry out all the words of the law.

> "The mystery was made known to me by revelation..." (Eph. 3:3, HCSB)

> "... as it is now revealed to His holy apostles and prophets by the Spirit:" (Eph. 3:5, HCSB)

The mysteries are the hidden secrets. They are revealed or brought to light by the Spirit. This revelation gives us working knowledge which we can apply to our lives and thereby become doers of God's word. This kind of lifestyle will result in true happiness that God wills for His people to have.

> "...but one who listens to instruction will be happy." (Pro. 29:18b, HCSB)

MYSTERY → REVELATION → KNOWLEDGE → OBEDIENCE → BLESSING

We need continuous revelation.

> "[17]I pray that the God of our Lord Jesus Christ, the glorious Father, would give you a spirit of wisdom and revelation in the knowledge of Him. [18]I pray that the perception of your mind may be enlightened so you may know what is the hope of His calling, what are the glorious riches of His inheritance among the saints, [19]and what is the immeasurable greatness of His power to us who believe, according to the working of His vast strength. [20]He demonstrated this power in the Messiah by raising Him from the dead and seating Him at His right hand in the heavens – [21]far above every ruler and authority, power and dominion, and every title given, not only in this age but also in the one to come. [22]And He put everything under His feet and appointed Him as head over everything for the church, [23] which is His body, the fullness of the One who fills all things in every way." (Eph. 1:17-23, HCSB)

This is a prayer I pray for myself. Unless we receive more of the Spirit of wisdom and revelation, how else will the eyes of our understanding be opened? How will believers know the purpose and the extent of our calling? Our finite minds cannot comprehend our great inheritance as children of God. The same Spirit of power that raised Christ from the dead lives in us! These great truths are spiritually grasped as the Spirit reveals them to our spirits. Once revelation explodes inside us, our minds will receive understanding of His thoughts, which are so much higher than our thoughts.

We will be as the Queen of Sheba after she saw Solomon's glory. She had previously heard of his fame. She did not believe these reports until she saw it with her own eyes. As she observed his wisdom, the extent of his immense wealth, his palace, his servants and his ministers' attire, her breath was taken away.

> "Howbeit I believed not the words, until I came, and mine eyes had seen it: and, behold, the half was not told me: thy wisdom and prosperity exceedeth the fame which I heard." (1 Kings 10:7, KJV)

Ask for the eyes of your understanding to be opened, I am certain you will be amazed by His riches and glory!

SECTION 4
THE ANOINTING

THE ANOINTING

The Hebrew word for 'anoint' is *mashakh*, which means to smear or spread a liquid.

> "²² The Lord spoke to Moses: ²³ "Take for yourself the finest spices: 12½ pounds of liquid myrrh, half as much (6¼ pounds) of fragrant cinnamon, 6¼ pounds of fragrant cane, ²⁴ 12½ pounds of cassia (by the sanctuary shekel), and one gallon of olive oil. ²⁵ Prepare from these a holy anointing oil, a scented blend, the work of a perfumer; it will be holy anointing oil." (Ex. 30: 22-25, HCSB)

The recipe for the holy perfumed oil called for the equivalent of 500 shekels of myrrh and cassia, 250 shekels of sweet cinnamon and cane, and a gallon of olive oil.

> "³² It must not be used for ordinary anointing on a person's body, and you must not make anything like it using its formula. It is holy, and it must be holy to you. ³³ Anyone who blends something like it or puts some of it on an unauthorized person must be cut off from his people." (Ex. 30: 32-33, HCSB)

The oil was holy, not ordinary. It was not meant to be used for any other purpose. Once something or someone was anointed, they were sanctified and set apart for God. The ordinary man was made holy. The Old Testament ritual of anointing with oil foreshadows the New Testament anointing of the Holy Spirit on all believers.

In the Bible, there are many instances of items that were anointed with oil – the tabernacle, the ark of the testimony, the table of shewbread, the candlestick, the altar of incense, and the laver, among others.

> "Consecrate them and they will be especially holy. Whatever touches them will be consecrated." (Ex. 30:29, HCSB)

The word 'sanctify' means to consecrate, sanctify, prepare, dedicate, be hallowed, be holy, be sanctified, or be separate. The action of anointing was done for the purpose of sanctification, consecration (to set apart), or the inauguration of a person into a new office. People who were anointed include the Messiah, Cyrus, Lucifer, Elisha the Prophet, Saul, David, and Solomon, as well as other Kings and Priests.

THE OIL AND PRIEST

THE ANOINTING OF PRIESTS

1 Peter 2:5 and 2:9 proclaim that we are a royal priesthood. We have much to learn by analogy in the consecration of the priests. God wants to set us apart to fulfill His will, so the same principles apply because the Old Testament is a shadow of the New Testament.

> "Anoint Aaron and his sons and consecrate them to serve Me as priests." (Ex. 30:30, HCSB)

Moses did as the Lord commanded him. The assembly was gathered together to the door of the tabernacle of the congregation. Moses washed Aaron and his sons with water. He put on their priestly garments. Moses anointed the tabernacle and the articles of worship.

> "He poured some of the anointing oil on Aaron's head and anointed and consecrated him." (Lev. 8:12, HCSB)

> "23Moses slaughtered it, took some of its blood, and put it on Aaron's right earlobe, on the thumb of his right hand, and on the big toe of his right foot. 24Moses also presented Aaron's sons and put some of the blood on their right earlobes, on the thumbs of their right hands, and on the big toes of their right feet. Then Moses sprinkled the blood on all sides of the altar." (Lev. 8:23-24, HCSB)

The priests were consecrated with the blood of the ram, implying that now they would hear, work, and walk differently. A ram was killed and its blood was poured out on the altar. This blood and the anointing oil were sprinkled on Aaron and his sons. This is a parallel to the New Testament 'priest' who is washed in the blood of Jesus and anointed with the Holy Spirit.

> "Then Moses took some of the anointing oil and some of the blood that was on the altar and sprinkled them on Aaron and his garments, as well as on his sons and their garments. In this way he consecrated Aaron and his garments, as well as his sons and their garments." (Lev. 8:30, HCSB)

> "How good and pleasant it is when brothers live together in harmony! 2 It is like fine oil on the head, running down on the beard, running down Aaron's beard onto his robes. 3 It is like the dew of Hermon falling on the mountains of Zion. For there the Lord has appointed the blessing – life forevermore." (Ps. 133:1-3, HCSB)

Aaron was no longer an ordinary man. A description of the anointing oil is given in Psalms 133, comparing the unity of the believers with the anointing oil, which is good and pleasant. The act of consecration takes ordinary people and sets them apart for God's purpose.

ANOINTING OF KINGS

"...and has made us kings and priests to His God and Father..." (Rev. 1:6, KJV)

Just as God anointed kings in the Old Testament, He has anointed us to be kings and priests under the new covenant. To understand the anointing better, one must study the anointing of kings in scripture.

SAUL

"Samuel took the flask of oil, poured it out on Saul's head, kissed him, and said, "Hasn't the Lord anointed you ruler over His inheritance?" (1 Sam. 10:1, HCSB)

Purpose of Saul's Anointing

"...Anoint him ruler over My people Israel. He will save them from the hand of the Philistines..." (1 Sam. 9:16, HCSB)

Saul was anointed with oil to be the first king of Israel. Shortly afterwards, the Holy Spirit fell upon him. Saul was anointed to fulfill God's purpose to rule the people of Israel as king and to destroy the Amalekites. Saul then disobeyed God, and God rejected him from being king over Israel.

"...the Lord was with David but had left Saul." (1 Sam. 18:12, HCSB)

In 1 Samuel 24, David has a chance to kill Saul, but he cut off the edge of his robe instead. David felt convicted of sin after this.

"He said to his men, "I swear before the Lord: I would never do such a thing to my lord, the Lord's anointed. I will never lift my hand against him, since he is the Lord's anointed." [7] With these words David persuaded his men, and he did not let them rise up against Saul. Then Saul left the cave and went on his way. [8] After that, David got up, went out of the cave, and called to Saul, "My lord the king!" When Saul looked behind him, David bowed to the ground in homage. [9] David said to Saul, "Why do you listen to the words of people who say, 'Look, David intends to harm you'?" (1 Sam. 24:6-9, HCSB)

David revered the anointing of God upon Saul, even after the Lord has departed from him. David had a reverent fear for the anointing of God. When Saul died, an Amalekite reported that he had killed Saul hoping to get some reward from David. David responded by saying, "How is it that you were not afraid to lift your hand to destroy the Lord's anointed?" (2 Sam. 1:14, HCSB) Saul died in battle, and David lamented his death.

"...for there the shield of the mighty was defiled – the shield of Saul, no longer anointed with oil." (2 Sam. 1: 21, HCSB)

David revered the anointing and did not take matters into his own hands. He waited for God to act. God poured out His vengeance on Saul and he was killed in battle.

Like David, we must have reverence for the anointing as it is the very tangible presence of God on the believer's life. We are but jars of clay with great treasure inside. It is a great mystery that Almighty God can dwell within frail creatures of dust. Even the heaven of heavens cannot contain Him, but He chooses to make His dwelling in us. Indeed, He is Immanuel, God with us.

DAVID

In 1 Samuel 16:1, God instructed Samuel to fill his horn with oil and to anoint as the next king, one of the sons of Jesse the Bethlehemite. Samuel saw each of the sons of Jesse, but neither of them was God's choice. David was presented to Samuel, and the Lord instructed Samuel to anoint him.

> "¹² So Jesse sent for him. He had beautiful eyes and a healthy, handsome appearance. Then the Lord said, "Anoint him, for he is the one." ¹³ So Samuel took the horn of oil, anointed him in the presence of his brothers, and the Spirit of the Lord took control of David from that day forward. Then Samuel set out and went to Ramah."
> (1 Sam. 16:12-13, HCSB)

Purpose of David's Anointing

Ps 78:70-72 shows us that God chose David to lead Israel like a shepherd leads a flock. He was meant to lead them with a pure heart and skillful hands.

The physical anointing with oil is followed by the spiritual anointing of the Holy Spirit. After this event, the insignificant David begins to undergo a transformation and preparation to take up the throne as a man after God's own heart. David was not summoned along with the other brothers. We are left to surmise that he was not as impressive in appearance as his brothers. David was called in from the field only because Samuel insisted on seeing him.

At the time of his anointing, David is described as ruddy, of a beautiful countenance, and goodly to look at. However, over the course of time, Saul asks for a skillful musician.

> "¹⁷Then Saul commanded his servants, "Find me someone who plays well and bring him to me." ¹⁸ One of the young men answered, "I have seen a son of Jesse of Bethlehem who knows how to play the lyre. He is also a valiant man, a warrior, eloquent, handsome, and the Lord is with him."" (1 Sam. 16: 17-18, HCSB)

In verse 18, a servant describes David, a son of Jesse the Bethlehemite, as being cunning in playing, a mighty valiant man, a man of war, prudent in matters, a comely person, and the Lord is with him. The anointing of the Holy Spirit seems to have blessed David in every aspect of his life and transformed him.

Skill: We see David plays so skillfully that the evil spirit departs from Saul. (1 Sam. 16:23, HCSB)

Might: The anointing enables him to defeat Goliath.

Wisdom: David conducted himself wisely in all his ways because the Lord was with him. (1 Sam. 18:14)

Favor: David earned the favor of all of Israel and Judah. (1 Sam. 18:16). David behaved more wisely than all the servants of Saul, so that his name became highly esteemed. (1 Sam. 18:30)

> "And the men of Judah came, and there they anointed David king over the house of Judah." (2 Sam. 2:4, HCSB)

After Saul's death, David inquired of the Lord. God asked him to go to Hebron in Judah. David ruled as king in Hebron for seven and a half years. In 2 Samuel 5:3, David was anointed king over all twelve tribes of Israel. He ruled for 33 years.

JEHU

Elisha instructed one of the prophets to anoint Jehu as the next king of Israel.

> "²When you get there, look for Jehu son of Jehoshaphat, son of Nimshi. Go in, get him away from his colleagues, and take him to an inner room. ³Then, take the flask of oil, pour it on his head, and say, 'This is what the Lord says: "I anoint you king over Israel."'" (2 Kings 9:2-3, HCSB)

Purpose of Jehu's Anointing

> "⁶So Jehu got up and went into the house. The young prophet poured the oil on his head and said, "This is what the LORD God of Israel says: 'I anoint you king over the Lord's people, Israel. ⁷You are to strike down the house of your master Ahab so that I may avenge the blood shed by the hand of Jezebel – the blood of My servants the prophets and of all the servants of the LORD.'" (2 Kings 9:6-7, HCSB)

Jehu tried to downplay the incident, saying that the prophets were strange people. His peers, however, instantly recognized Jehu as king.

"Each man quickly took his garment and put it under Jehu on the bare steps. They blew the ram's horn and proclaimed, "Jehu is king!" (2 Kings 9:13, HCSB)

People recognized the anointing on Jehu. The anointing is received when we get away with God in that inner chamber. We are anointed to fulfill God's will and purpose for our generation. Those anointed receive great favor and must remember to give all the glory to God.

ELIJAH'S MANTLE

ELISHA

Elijah the prophet was instructed by God to appoint Elisha as his successor.

> "You are to anoint … Elisha son of Shaphat from Abel-meholah as prophet in your place." (1 Kings 19:16, HCSB)

THE ANOINTING OF ELISHA

Elijah found Elisha plowing a field.

> "Elijah left there and found Elisha son of Shaphat as he was plowing. Twelve teams of oxen were in front of him, and he was with the twelfth team. Elijah walked by him and threw his mantle over him." (1 Kings 19:19, HCSB)

Elijah's mantle was not just a regular cloak, but was a mantle associated with power. The Hebrew word used here for cloak is *addereth*, which means 'glory' or 'cloak'.

It is interesting to note that Elijah did not anoint Elisha with oil; instead he cast his mantle upon him as God had directed. A prophet's garment represented his authority. Elijah's mantle was not mere fabric, but a tangible representation imbued with 'power'.

The English word 'mantle' is used to translate three different Hebrew words – *Semikiyah*, *Meheel*, and *Addereth*.

1. *SEMIKIYAH - RUG*

> "Jael went out to greet Sisera and said to him, "Come in, my lord. Come in with me. Don't be afraid." So he went into her tent, and she covered him with a rug." (Judg. 4:18, HCSB)

2. *MEHEEL - COMMON OUTER CLOAK OR GARMENT*

> "When Samuel turned to go, Saul grabbed the hem of his robe, and it tore." (1 Sam. 15:27, HCSB)

3. *ADDERETH – AN OUTER GARMENT*

Addereth signifies an outer garment, but is from a root word meaning 'power'. This is used to refer to Elijah's mantle. It is associated with glory, splendor, and magnificence. Elijah's mantle was like the rod of Moses. On its own it was an ordinary object. When God used it, it became an instrument of power. The object was not meant to be worshipped. It was an outward symbol of a spiritual truth.

At the end of Elijah's time on earth, just before he was taken up in the chariot of fire, Elisha made a bold request of him. Elisha asked for a double portion of the spirit that Elijah had!

> "⁸ Elijah took his mantle, rolled it up, and struck the waters, which parted to the right and left. Then the two of them crossed over on dry ground. ⁹After they had crossed over, Elijah said to Elisha, "Tell me what I can do for you before I am taken from you." So Elisha answered, "Please, let me inherit two shares of your spirit." ¹⁰ Elijah replied, "You have asked for something difficult. If you see me being taken from you, you will have it. If not, you won't." (2 Kings 2:8-10, HCSB)

Elijah stated that this was a difficult thing to attain, considering that during this time the Spirit was not poured out on all flesh – only upon certain prophets and priests for certain causes and for specific durations. Elijah said that Elisha would receive the double portion if he saw him when being taken up to heaven.

> "¹¹As they continued walking and talking, a chariot of fire with horses of fire suddenly appeared and separated the two of them. Then Elijah went up into heaven in the whirlwind. ¹²As Elisha watched, he kept crying out, "My father, my father, the chariots and horsemen of Israel!" Then he never saw Elijah again. He took hold of his own clothes and tore them into two pieces. ¹³Elisha picked up the mantle that had fallen off Elijah and went back and stood on the bank of the Jordan. ¹⁴Then he took the mantle Elijah had dropped and struck the waters. "Where is the Lord God of Elijah?" he asked. He struck the waters himself, and they parted to the right and the left, and Elisha crossed over." (2 Kings 2:11-14, HCSB)

When Elijah was taken up, Elisha tore his own clothes and took up the mantle of Elijah. Once Elisha wore the mantle of Elijah, he was no longer an apprentice. His first miracle was to part the waters just as Elijah had performed in verse 8, of parting the waters in two and crossing over the river. The prophets clearly recognized Elisha as Elijah's successor saying that "The spirit of Elijah doth rest upon Elisha."

In keeping with his request, Elisha did twice as many miracles as Elijah had done. We need to earnestly seek a greater anointing just as Elisha did.

> "For God sent Him, and He speaks God's words, since He gives the Spirit **without measure**." (John 3:34, HCSB)

In the church age, God is pouring His Spirit upon all flesh, not only upon prophets and kings. God is willing to give us more than the double portion, as long as we desire and seek after the anointing as Elisha did. God is willing to give us as much as we are willing to take. The more space we make for Him, the greater amount of His Presence we can contain. We are the temples of the Holy Ghost, and just as the glory filled the Old Testament temple, the same glory can fill us.

> "...so you may be filled with all the fullness of God. Now to Him who is able to do above and beyond all that we ask or think according to the power that works in us..." (Eph. 3:19-20, HCSB)

CYRUS: THE LORD'S ANOINTED

"The Lord says this to Cyrus, His anointed, whose right hand I have grasped to subdue nations before him, to disarm kings, to open the doors before him and the gates will not be shut..." (Isa. 45:1, HCSB)

Cyrus the Great was a Persian king of the Medo-Persian Empire that conquered Babylon. Why was he anointed of God? Why did God want him to subdue nations? Many kings in history have done this. What made Cyrus so special? Why did God bestow His anointing on him?

The history of this story starts in Deuteronomy 28:45-52 and 62-65. These passages describe the curses associated with disobedience to the Law and not hearkening to the voice of God. God warned Israel that if it disobeyed His Law, it would be attacked by a fierce nation that would besiege its gates and bring great destruction. When the people of Israel walked in disobedience, these curses came into effect. God gave them many warnings, but they gave no heed and persisted in idolatry and disobedience.

In 2 Chronicles 36:5-23, the Babylonians attacked Judah. Under the leadership of Judah's previous three kings, Jerusalem had been besieged - its Temple treasures carried off to Babylon. With each siege came further destruction. God sent His prophets to warn them.

"[14]All the leaders of the priests and the people multiplied their unfaithful deeds, imitating all the detestable practices of the nations, and they defiled the Lord's temple that He had consecrated in Jerusalem. [15]But Yahweh, the God of their ancestors sent word against them by the hand of His messengers, sending them time and time again, for He had compassion on His people and on His dwelling place. [16] But they kept ridiculing God's messengers, despising His words, and scoffing at His prophets, until the Lord's wrath was so stirred up against His people that there was no remedy. [17]So He brought up against them the king of the Chaldeans, who killed their choice young men with the sword in the house of their sanctuary. He had no pity on young men or young women, elderly or aged; He handed them all over to him. [18]He took everything to Babylon – all the articles of God's temple, large and small, the treasures of the Lord's temple, and the treasures of the king and his officials. [19]Then the Chaldeans burned God's temple. They tore down Jerusalem's wall, burned down all its palaces, and destroyed all its valuable articles. [20]He deported those who escaped from the sword to Babylon, and they became servants to him and his sons until the rise of the Persian kingdom." (2 Chron. 36: 14-20, HCSB)

All the priceless vessels of the temple were taken away. The people were killed and carried away to Babylon. The temple was burnt down and the walls were broken down. Judah was defenseless and desolate. Judah remained like this for 70 years according to the prophecy of Jeremiah.

God does not leave His people desolate. The end of the chapter talks of the promise of restoration, in which God appointed a foreign king and anointed him to conquer the Babylonians. God charged Cyrus to build the temple in Jerusalem, and anointed him to initiate the rebuilding of the desolate Jerusalem.

CYRUS' EDICT

> "²²In the first year of Cyrus king of Persia, the word of the Lord spoken through Jeremiah was fulfilled. The Lord put it into the mind of King Cyrus of Persia to issue a proclamation throughout his entire kingdom and also to put it in writing: ²³This is what King Cyrus of Persia says: The Lord, the God of heaven, has given me all the kingdoms of the earth and has appointed me to build Him a temple at Jerusalem in Judah. Whoever among you of His people may go up, and may the Lord his God be with him." (2 Chron. 36:22-23, HCSB)

Cyrus was a tool in the hand of the master builder. It was God's idea to rebuild Jerusalem.

> "Who says to Cyrus, "My shepherd, he will fulfill all My pleasure" and says to Jerusalem, "She will be rebuilt," and of the temple, "Its foundation will be laid." (Isa. 44:28, HCSB)

> "The Lord says this to Cyrus, His anointed, whose right hand I have grasped to subdue nations before him, to disarm kings, to open the doors before him and the gates will not be shut" (Isa. 45:1, HCSB)

History records that the night the Medes and the Persians attacked Babylon, Belshazzar was hosting a great party and the gates to the fortress were not shut as they should have been. They were wide open and Belshazzar was overthrown.

Babylon had kept the exiles and the temple treasures for seventy years. So God replaced Belshazzar with the Medo-Persians. They were used by God to return the exiles to Jerusalem and begin its restoration.

> "I have raised him up in righteousness, and will level all roads for him. He will rebuild My city, and set My exiles free, not for a price or a bribe says the Lord of Hosts." (Isa. 45:13, HCSB)

It is interesting to note that the law of the Medes and the Persians could not be reversed. Once a decree was made, it had to be fulfilled. Many years later, when the Jews encountered opposition to the temple rebuilding, they asked the ruling king to pull up the ancient records of Cyrus. Once the king found the decree, the rebuilding of Jerusalem was allowed to continue without further hindrance.

HISTORICAL SIGNIFICANCE

The proclamation for rebuilding is pivotal in Jewish history. The edict to rebuild Jerusalem marks the beginning of the 70 weeks of Daniel. The Messiah was cut off 62 weeks after this event.

> "Know and understand this: From the issuing of the decree to restore and rebuild Jerusalem until Messiah the Prince will be seven weeks and 62 weeks. It will be rebuilt with a plaza and a moat, but in difficult times." (Dan. 9:25, HCSB)

The purpose of the anointing is to enable us to do God's pleasure and to fulfill His will in our generation. We are but a tool in the hand of the master builder.

LUCIFER: THE ANOINTED CHERUB

LAW OF DOUBLE REFERENCE

A single prophecy may have more than one meaning, or it may refer to two separate events or persons. You can discern if this law is being used when the scripture addresses a real person, but certain statements also refer to an invisible being with the same characteristics. Certain statements in a passage refer to one person or event, while some refer to another, describing a historic scenario and a future prophecy. Since the historic portion is obviously accurate, you can be sure the prophetic portion will also come to pass.

There are many instances in scripture where this principle needs to be applied. Let us look at facts about Lucifer from Ezekiel 28.

> "[12] "Son of man, lament for the king of Tyre and say to him: This is what the Lord God says: You were the seal of perfection, full of wisdom and perfect in beauty. [13] You were in Eden, the garden of God. Every kind of precious stone covered you: carnelian, topaz, and diamond, beryl, onyx, and jasper, sapphire, turquoise and emerald. Your mountings and settings were crafted in gold; they were prepared on the day you were created. [14] You were an anointed guardian cherub, for I had appointed you. You were on the holy mountain of God; you walked among the fiery stones. [15] From the day you were created you were blameless in your ways until wickedness was found in you. [16] Through the abundance of your trade, you were filled with violence, and you sinned. So I expelled you in disgrace from the mountain of God, and banished you, guardian cherub, from among the fiery stones. [17] Your heart became proud because of your beauty; For the sake of your splendor you corrupted your wisdom. So I threw you down to the earth; I made you a spectacle before kings. [18] You profaned your sanctuaries by the magnitude of your iniquities in your dishonest trade. So I made fire come from within you, and it consumed you. I reduced you to ashes on the ground in the sight of everyone watching you."" (Ezek. 28:12-18, HCSB)

Certain parts of this passage refer to Lucifer or Satan, while others are applicable to the mortal king of Tyre. Verse 13 says "You were in Eden." This cannot possibly refer to the mortal king of Tyre; hence, we infer that it refers to Lucifer. Verses 12-14 describe Lucifer as a created being of perfection, beauty, and as being covered with precious stones.

THE CHERUBIM

Satan was an angelic being, but he was not just a regular angel. He was a cherub, part of the collective cherubim. The cherubim are the angels that stand right in front of the throne of God.

They minister to Him continually and are the closest to His presence. They are first mentioned in Genesis in Eden after the Fall.

> "He drove man out and stationed the cherubim and the flaming, whirling sword east of the Garden of Eden to guard the way to the tree of life." (Gen. 3:24, HCSB)

These cherubim illustrated the fact that the way to the presence of God was indeed guarded. Any human flesh attempting to enter and partake of the tree of life would be cut down by the sword. This is also seen in the lives of Nadab and Abihu, who approached the Lord with strange fire and were consumed. Uzzah tried to steady the ark as the oxen stumbled. He was killed because no flesh could approach the presence of the Lord without an atoning sacrifice.

> "...You who sit enthroned on the cherubim, rise up." (Ps. 80:1, HCSB)

This physical representation of the cherubim is a type of the true picture in heaven, for God is surrounded by the cherubim and seraphim. In the tabernacle, two cherubim overshadow the mercy seat on the Ark of the Covenant. In Solomon's temple, the ark was placed under the wings of two massive golden cherubim in the Most Holy place. The veil of the temple was made with cherubim skillfully embroidered into it. The veil barred people from entering and seeing the Holiest Place. Jesus paid the atonement price by His death. By the blood of Jesus, we are able to enter the Holiest Place.

> "...by a new and living way He has opened for us through the curtain (that is, His flesh) ..." (Heb. 10:20, HCSB)

The point to be remembered is that Lucifer was one of these anointed, covering cherubs. This was as close as anyone could get to the Presence of the Lord. This was one of the highest 'positions' any angel could get. He then went on to lose his position as the anointed cherub.

> "[15]From the day you were created you were blameless in your ways until wickedness was found in you. [16]Through the abundance of your trade, you were filled with violence, and you sinned. So I expelled you in disgrace from the mountain of God, and banished you, guardian cherub, from among the fiery stones. [17]Your heart became proud because of your beauty; For the sake of your splendor you corrupted your wisdom. So I threw you down to the earth; I made you a spectacle before kings." (Ezek. 28:15-17, HCSB)

Lucifer was a covering cherub until the day he sinned. His beauty had caused him to become proud, and pride corrupted his wisdom. Lucifer was expelled and then cast out of heaven after he committed treason.

> "Shining morning star, how you have fallen from the heavens! You destroyer of nations, you have been cut down to the ground." (Isa. 14:12, HCSB)

Here Lucifer is called the morning star, son of the dawn. The phrase, 'you have been cut down' is depicted by the word *gada*, which means to be hewn or chopped down like a tree.

THE 'I' WILL

> "¹³You said to yourself: "I will ascend to the heavens; I will set up my throne above the stars of God. I will sit on the mount of the gods' assembly, in the remotest parts of the North. ¹⁴ I will ascend above the highest clouds; I will make myself like the Most High."(Isa. 14:13-14, HCSB)

The interesting thing is that the devil tempts us with the same ideas. He deceived Eve telling her she could be like God if she ate the forbidden fruit. We must not succumb to the same temptation as the devil. Lucifer did not value what he had. He let pride get in the way. We need to treasure our position and anointing in Christ.

MESSIAH: THE ANOINTED ONE

"You love righteousness and hate wickedness; therefore God, your God, has anointed you with the oil of joy more than your companions." (Ps. 45:7, HCSB)

We know that the Hebrew word for 'anoint' is *mashakh*, which means to smear or to spread a liquid. The word 'Messiah' is derived from the Hebrew word *meshiyach*, which means 'Anointed One'.

"Then a shoot will grow from the stump of Jesse, and a branch from his roots will bear fruit. ² The Spirit of the Lord will rest on Him – a Spirit of wisdom and understanding, a Spirit of counsel and strength, a Spirit of knowledge and of the fear of the Lord. ³ His delight will be in the fear of the Lord. He will not judge by what He sees with His eyes, He will not execute justice by what He hears with His ears, ⁴ but He will judge the poor righteously and execute justice for the oppressed of the land. He will strike the land with discipline from His mouth, and He will kill the wicked with a command from His lips." (Isa. 11: 1-4, HCSB)

This is a prophecy in Isaiah about the Spirit of God being on Jesus. In verse 3 of Isaiah 11, we see the sevenfold characteristics of the Holy Spirit. Jesus was **full** of the Holy Spirit, so **all** these characteristics were seen in Him.

THE ANOINTING OF JESUS

Priests (Aaron) and kings (David) were anointed with oil. Elisha was anointed when Elijah cast his mantle on him. This was just a physical representation of the Holy Spirit coming upon them.

When and How Was Jesus Anointed?

"After Jesus was baptized, He went up immediately from the water. The heavens suddenly opened for Him, and He saw the Spirit of God descending like a dove and coming down on Him." (Matt. 3:16, HCSB)

The Holy Spirit is not a literal dove, but He chose to be seen as a dove descending on Jesus.

How Much of The Anointing Did Jesus Receive?

"For God sent Him, and He speaks God's words, since He gives the Spirit without measure." (John 3:34, HCSB)

Jesus was anointed with the Holy Ghost without limit.

"Then Jesus returned from the Jordan, full of the Holy Spirit, and was led by the Spirit in the wilderness." (Luke 4:1, HCSB)

Jesus went into the wilderness full of the Spirit, fasted for 40 days, and then returned from the wilderness.

"Then Jesus returned to Galilee in the power of the Spirit, and news about Him spread throughout the entire vicinity." (Luke 4:14, HCSB)

"The scroll of the prophet Isaiah was given to Him…" (Luke 4:17, HCSB)

Luke 4:17 records how Jesus went to the synagogue. He read the scroll as was the custom. Jesus read Isaiah 61, and then sat down.

The Purpose of The Anointing

"The Spirit of the Lord God is on Me, because the Lord has anointed Me to bring good news to the poor. He has sent Me to heal the brokenhearted, to proclaim liberty to the captives and freedom to the prisoners; ² to proclaim the year of the Lord's favor, and the day of our God's vengeance; to comfort all who mourn, ³ to provide for those who mourn in Zion; to give them a crown of beauty instead of ashes, festive oil instead of mourning, and splendid clothes instead of despair. And they will be called righteous trees, planted by the Lord to glorify Him." (Isa. 61:1-3, HCSB)

In Isaiah 61:2, we see Jesus proclaiming the acceptable year of the Lord. This alludes to the Jubilee in Leviticus 25.

THE JUBILEE

This is the 50th year. A trumpet was used to proclaim this special occasion. In this year, all mortgages were cancelled, all debts forgiven, all servants released, and all lands were returned to their original owners.

"You are to consecrate the fiftieth year and proclaim freedom in the land for all its inhabitants. It will be your Jubilee, when each of you is to return to his property and each of you to his clan." (Lev. 25:10, HCSB)

This is exactly what Jesus did for us. When Jesus came back from the wilderness, He started His public ministry. He healed the sick, raised the dead, and set people free. He came intending to die. Through His death He redeemed all the sons of Adam from Satan, who were held in bondage since the fall of man. Jesus is our kinsman redeemer, who paid for our debt and set us free to return to God.

"[14]Now since the children have flesh and blood in common, Jesus also shared in these, so that through His death He might destroy the one holding the power of death – that is, the Devil – [15] and free those who were held in slavery all their lives by the fear of death." (Heb. 2: 14-15, HCSB)

After suffering in death, Jesus descended to the Underworld (*Sheol*) and took the keys of Hell and Death. Until then, all men, whether righteous or wicked, were held in the Underworld. Until the time of Christ, Death had the final say. The Messiah or 'Anointed One' was the first to defeat Death and be resurrected, never to die again. Believers now have this same hope – that they will be raised just like Christ was. Those that are alive will be translated after the dead in Christ rise. Death will not be able to hold us down.

SECTION 5

AN EXCELLENT SPIRIT

AN EXCELLENT SPIRIT

EXCELLENCE

The word 'excel' has a multitude of implications. It can mean to eclipse, transcend, exceed, top, beat, outdo, surpass, be better than others, be superior in achievement, quality, attainment, or performance.

> "³Reuben, you are my firstborn, my strength and the firstfruits of my virility, excelling in prominence, excelling in power. ⁴Turbulent as water, you will no longer excel, because you got into your father's bed and you defiled it – he got into my bed." (Gen. 49:3-4, HCSB)

Reuben was the firstborn of Jacob. The blessing and birthright belonged to him as the firstborn son. Coupled with it was the ability to excel, as the birthright gave him the preeminence in dignity and power.

YETHER

The word 'excellency' in Gen 49:3 in the King James Version is the Hebrew word *yether*. This means abundance, affluence, preeminence, or that which exceeds measure or limit. This word is also used to describe a cord, a rope, a string of a bow or harp, or a cord used as a bridle. These cords are all meant to be strong and taut. The symbolism implies a lack of slack. Their very purpose is to be tight or well-tuned.

Reuben forfeited his birthright when he slept with Jacob's concubine in Genesis 35:22. On his deathbed, Jacob blessed his sons, but Reuben received quite the opposite. Jacob cursed him and said, "…turbulent as water, you will no longer excel." (Gen. 49:4, HCSB)

THE PRIVILEGES OF THE FIRSTBORN

The genealogy was reckoned through the firstborn son. He received the double portion of the inheritance, as well as his father's blessing. The firstborn was bestowed with the right to lead the family.

> "These were the sons of Reuben the firstborn of Israel. He was the firstborn, but his birthright was given to the sons of Joseph son of Israel, because Reuben defiled his father's bed. He is not listed in the genealogy according to birthright. ²Although Judah became strong among his brothers and a ruler came from him, the birthright was given to Joseph." (1 Chron. 5:1-2, HCSB)

Judah received the right to lead the family when Reuben lost his blessing. Simeon and Levi too lost this blessing when they killed the men of Shechem in their anger. Although he was the fourth son, Judah earned this right instead. Joseph received the birthright, and the genealogy was recorded in Joseph's name in Genesis 37:2. When Joseph received the birthright, he received the blessing of Excellence. Joseph received the double portion of the inheritance in Genesis 48:21. This author's theory on as to why Joseph received the birthright is because he was the other 'firstborn' son from Jacob's other wife (Rachel).

AN EXCELLENT SPIRIT

> "²⁷ He that hath knowledge spareth his words: and a man of **understanding** is of an **excellent** spirit." (Pro. 17:27, KJV)

A man of understanding (*bene*) is of an excellent (*yakar*) spirit. *Yakar* implies something valuable, prized, weighty, precious, rare, or splendid. The excellent spirit is rare and not seen in regular men. Excellence is an attribute of the Holy Spirit. If we listen to Him, we will hear Him speak of excellent things!

TWO TYPES OF WISDOM

There are two kinds of wisdom – *Bene* and *Khakam*. *Bene* is a Hebrew word which means God-given wisdom in contrast to earthly wisdom and experience. *Khakam* is wisdom that is gained through learning and experience. It is skillful, learned and prudent. *Bene* wisdom is a heavenly wisdom, while *Khakam* wisdom is human wisdom. *Bene* will cause the Christian to stand apart and be distinct. While human wisdom is not to be undervalued, it is obvious that *Bene* transcends *Khakam*, just as the heavens are higher than the earth.

JOSEPH

> "So now, let Pharaoh look for a discerning and wise man and set him over the land of Egypt." (Gen. 41:33, HCSB)

Here, the discerning (*bene*) and wise (*khakam*) man is set over the land of Egypt.

> "³⁸Then Pharaoh said to his servants, "Can we find anyone like this, a man who has God's spirit in him?" ³⁹So Pharaoh said to Joseph, "Since God has made all this known to you, there is no one as intelligent and wise as you are." (Gen. 41:38-39, HCSB)

The *bene* wisdom of God in Joseph caused him to stand apart or be distinguished from the rest of the magicians in Pharaoh's court. All the other wise men had *khakam*, but Joseph was blessed with both *bene* and *khakam*. Gen 41 talks of Pharaoh's troubling dream about the coming famine in Egypt. Joseph was able to explain the dream because he had *bene*. He was a man with an excellent spirit.

SOLOMON

"So give Your servant an obedient heart to judge Your people and to discern between good and evil. For who is able to judge this great people of Yours?" (1 Kings 3:9, HCSB)

"I will therefore do what you have asked. I will give you a wise and understanding heart, so that there has never been anyone like you before and never will be again."
(1 Kings 3:12, HCSB)

When Solomon asked for heavenly or *bene* wisdom, God gave him the earthly or *khakam* wisdom too.

"Solomon's wisdom was greater than the wisdom of all the people of the East, greater than all the wisdom of Egypt." (1 Kings 4:30, HCSB)

Needless to say, that Godly wisdom exceeds all earthly wisdom. This is available to us as we commune with God. As the deep calls to the deep, a transfer of wisdom will happen as our spirit communes with His.

BEZALEL AND AHOLIAB

"Bezalel, Oholiab, and all the skilled people are to work based on everything the Lord has commanded. The Lord has given them wisdom and understanding to know how to do all the work of constructing the sanctuary." (Ex. 36:1, HCSB)

Bezalel and Aholiab needed the skill and experience of man as well as the wisdom of God to make the articles of the Tabernacle according to the pattern given to Moses. They needed to be able to discern and comprehend what Moses was telling them and create it with outstanding craftsmanship. When the tabernacle was complete, it was made just as God had commanded it to be made. They could not have done this without *bene* and *khakam*.

We too can excel if we have the Spirit of God in us. Both *bene* and *khakam* are available to us so we can excel and glorify the Lord who gives us His Excellent Spirit.

DANIEL

In the story about the handwriting on the wall in Daniel 5, Belshazzar called all his wise men to read the writing and decipher it.

> "So all the king's wise men came in, but none could read the inscription or make its interpretation known to him." (Dan. 5:8, HCSB)

The queen mother then told the king about Daniel who had served his grandfather.

> "There is a man in your kingdom who has the spirit of the holy gods in him. In the days of your predecessor he was found to have insight, intelligence, and wisdom like the wisdom of the gods. Your predecessor, King Nebuchadnezzar, appointed him chief of the diviners, mediums, Chaldeans, and astrologers. Your own predecessor, the king..." (Dan. 5:11, HCSB)

She recognized that there was something supernatural about this man, and that he had wisdom which was not common to man because in him was this 'Spirit of the Holy Gods'. The queen recollects and enumerates all of Daniel's exceptional qualities.

> "Forasmuch as an **excellent** spirit, and knowledge, and understanding, interpreting of dreams, and shewing of hard sentences, and dissolving of doubts, were found in the same Daniel, whom the king named Belteshazzar: now let Daniel be called, and he will shew the interpretation." (Dan. 5:12, KJV)

The word 'excellent' is the word *yattiyr*, which is derived from the Hebrew word *yakar*. It means pre-eminent, surpassing, extreme, extraordinary, or very great. The king sent for Daniel, and he read the writing and explained that the kingdom would be overthrown by the Medes and Persians. That night this prophecy came to pass and King Belshazzar was executed. Even unbelievers recognized that Daniel had the Spirit of God in him. This is what set him apart from the crowd. Even in his old age, Daniel was extraordinary.

> "I've heard that you have the spirit of the gods in you, and that you have insight, intelligence, and extraordinary wisdom." (Dan. 5:14, HCSB)

This is what King Belshazzar spoke to Daniel after he summoned him to his court.

> "Do you see a man skilled in his work? He will stand in the presence of kings. He will not stand in the presence of unknown men." (Pro. 22:29, HCSB)

Even though Daniel was unknown to King Belshazzar, it was his gift and wisdom that brought him before the presence of the king. Daniel did not purposefully call attention to himself. God shone the spotlight on him.

"A gift opens doors for a man and brings him before the great." (Pro. 18:16, HCSB)

This godly wisdom from the Holy Spirit caused Daniel to lead an exemplary life. His life was a sweet savor to God.

"³Daniel distinguished himself above the administrators and satraps because he had an extraordinary spirit, so the king planned to set him over the whole realm. ⁴The administrators and satraps, therefore, kept trying to find a charge against Daniel regarding the kingdom. But they could find no charge or corruption, for he was trustworthy, and no negligence or corruption was found in him." (Dan. 6:3-4, HCSB)

TEN TIMES BETTER

King Nebuchadnezzar asked his servants to find men to serve him. They were to possess the following traits.

"…young men without any physical defect, good-looking, suitable for instruction in all wisdom, knowledgeable, perceptive, and capable of serving in the king's palace – and to teach them the Chaldean language and literature." (Dan. 1:4, HCSB)

These young people were outstanding as a result of the hand of the Lord upon their lives.

"God gave these four young men knowledge (*khakam*) and understanding (*bene*) in every kind of literature and wisdom. Daniel also understood visions and dreams of every kind." (Dan. 1:17, HCSB)

"¹⁹ The king interviewed them, and among all of them, no one was found equal to Daniel, Hananiah, Mishael, and Azariah. So they began to serve in the king's court. ²⁰In every matter of wisdom and understanding that the king consulted them about, he found them ten times better than all the diviner-priests and mediums in his entire kingdom. (Dan. 1:19- 20, HCSB)

Note that Daniel and his friends stood apart from the rest of the crowd. They were ten times better. They surpassed, outdid, and beat the others. This is the very definition of the word 'excel'. They excelled because God gave them the knowledge and skill to do so.

THE FIRST DREAM

In Daniel 2, King Nebuchadnezzar has a dream which no one could tell or interpret. The king commanded that all the wise men be killed on account of their ineptitude. Daniel and his friends sought God's face for an answer.

> "18...urging them to ask the God of heaven for mercy concerning this mystery, so Daniel and his friends would not be killed with the rest of Babylon's wise men. 19 The mystery was then revealed to Daniel in a vision at night, and Daniel praised the God of heaven" (Dan. 2:18-19, HCSB)

> "26 The king said in reply to Daniel, whose name was Belteshazzar, "Are you able to tell me the dream I had and its interpretation?" 27 Daniel answered the king: "No wise man, medium, diviner-priest, or astrologer is able to make known to the king the mystery he asked about... 28 But there is a God in heaven who reveals mysteries, and He has let King Nebuchadnezzar know what will happen in the last days. Your dream and the visions that came into your mind as you lay in bed were these..." (Dan. 2:26-28, HCSB)

The purpose of Daniel's gift was to show the world that there is a God in heaven. God used Daniel's gift to reveal Himself to a heathen kingdom. Daniel did not take any glory for himself. The greater measure of the Holy Spirit that we have, the more humility we should have. The more awareness that we have of His awesomeness should bring humility as we realize that we are nothing, and have nothing, and can do nothing without Him.

> "29 ...The revealer of mysteries has let you know what will happen. 30 As for me, this mystery has been revealed to me, not because I have more wisdom than anyone living..." (Dan. 2:29-30, HCSB)

Daniel interpreted the dream for the king.

> "The king said to Daniel, "Your God is indeed God of gods, Lord of kings, and a revealer of mysteries, since you were able to reveal this mystery." (Dan. 2:47, HCSB)

> "A gift opens doors for a man and brings him before the great." (Pro. 18:16, HCSB)

DANIEL'S GIFT - THE INTERPRETATION OF DREAMS

The purpose of Daniel's gift was to show that there is a God in heaven. The use of this gift also brought two things – promotion and reward.

> "Then the king promoted Daniel and gave him many generous gifts. He made him ruler over the entire province of Babylon and chief governor over all the wise men of Babylon." (Dan. 2:48, HCSB)

The king made Daniel a great man, gave him many great gifts, and made him ruler over the whole province of Babylon, as well as chief of the governors over all the wise men of Babylon.

THE SECOND DREAM

Nebuchadnezzar had another dream which troubled him. He called for all his wise men and soothsayers. None of them were able to interpret the dream.

> "⁸ Finally Daniel, named Belteshazzar after the name of my god – and the spirit of the holy gods is in him – came before me. I told him the dream: ⁹"Belteshazzar, head of the diviners, because I know that you have a spirit of the holy gods and that no mystery puzzles you, explain to me the visions of my dream that I saw, and its interpretation."" (Dan. 4:8-9, HCSB)

Daniel is never seen pushing his way to the front. He was not an attention seeker, yet he ended up in the limelight because of his gift and exceptional wisdom. He did not run after promotion, but he was made master of the magicians and later the third ruler in the kingdom. In each of these events, even though Daniel was called upon to perform a humanly impossible task, he was able to fulfill the king's request. Daniel was so filled with God's Spirit that he could do what other men could not.

> "…Now, Belteshazzar, tell me the interpretation, because none of the wise men of my kingdom can make the interpretation known to me. But you can, because you have the spirit of the holy gods." (Dan. 4:18, HCSB)

Oh, that we would be full of this Excellent Spirit! Though we may not stand before kings, we are called to shine God's light to all those in our spheres of influence who live in darkness. Daniel's life showed an ungodly nation that there is a God in heaven. If we ever end up in the limelight, may we be like Daniel, who turned the spotlight right back to God. May the fullness of the Spirit bring us the humility that Daniel possessed.

"He that hath knowledge spareth his words: and a man of understanding is of an excellent spirit." (Pro. 17:27, NKJV)

Although it is not explicitly written that Joseph had an excellent spirit like Daniel, he was recognized as a man in whom the Spirit of God lived. Joseph exhibited the same characteristics as Daniel. We also saw earlier that Joseph received the birthright which Reuben forfeited. This birthright gave Joseph the ability to excel. Remember Gen 49:3? The birthright gave the firstborn the excellency of power and dignity – the ability to excel. Joseph also had the same gift of interpretation of dreams as Daniel.

"Do you see a man skilled in his work? He will stand in the presence of kings. He will not stand in the presence of unknown men." (Pro. 22: 29, HCSB)

DILIGENT

"²The Lord was with Joseph, and he became a successful man, serving in the household of his Egyptian master. ³When his master saw that the Lord was with him and that the Lord made everything he did successful…" (Gen. 39:2-3, HCSB)

Joseph was a hard-working individual of impeccable character and integrity. Combine this with God's favor, and it is a formula for success.

Joseph's career had a pattern. He rose up the ladder in every situation in which he is placed – Potiphar's house, the prison, and the palace. He was cast down many times (starting at the pit), but would not remain there. He was perpetually moving forward and upward.

PROMOTION #1

"⁴Joseph found favor in his master's sight and became his personal attendant. Potiphar also put him in charge of his household and placed all that he owned under his authority. ⁵From the time that he put him in charge of his household and of all that he owned, the Lord blessed the Egyptian's house because of Joseph. The Lord's blessing was on all that he owned, in his house and in his fields. ⁶He left all that he owned under Joseph's authority; he did not concern himself with anything except the food he ate. Now Joseph was well-built and handsome." (Gen. 39:4-6, HCSB)

FAITHFUL

When Potiphar's wife tempted him, Joseph said in Genesis 39:9, "How then can I do this great wickedness, and sin against God?" Joseph was faithful even when no one was watching. Potiphar's wife accused him unjustly and he was thrown into jail. Though it seemed like all was lost for Joseph, God was working out His plans to exalt him.

> "But the Lord was with Joseph and extended kindness to him. He granted him favor in the eyes of the prison warden." (Gen. 39:21, HCSB)

PROMOTION #2

> "²²The warden put all the prisoners who were in the prison under Joseph's authority, and he was responsible for everything that was done there. ²³The warden did not bother with anything under Joseph's authority, because the Lord was with him, and the Lord made everything that he did successful." (Gen. 39:22-23, HCSB)

Joseph was so good at his work that both his bosses left everything to his care. He was trustworthy.

> "A gift opens doors for a man and brings him before the great." (Pro. 18:16, HCSB)

JOSEPH'S GIFT

Like Daniel, Joseph had the gift of interpretation of dreams. While in prison, two of the prisoners had dreams. They were upset as there was no one to interpret the dreams for them. Joseph addressed them.

> "…Joseph said to them, "Don't interpretations belong to God? Tell me your dreams." (Gen. 40:8, HCSB)

Joseph interpreted the dream of Pharaoh's cupbearer.

> "When the chief baker saw that the interpretation was positive, he said to Joseph, "I also had a dream…." (Gen. 40:16, HCSB)

Joseph interpreted his dream as well. Three days later, both the dreams and their interpretations came to pass. Two years later, Pharaoh had two dreams which troubled him.

> "When morning came, he was troubled, so he summoned all the magicians of Egypt and all its wise men. Pharaoh told them his dreams, but no one could interpret them for him." (Gen. 41:8, HCSB)

Does this sound familiar? This is the same situation as in Daniel's time. God is setting the stage for Joseph to show another pagan king that there is a God in heaven. Scripture tell us that Joseph was kept in prison till the 'right time'.

> "Until the time his prediction came true, the word of the Lord tested him."
> (Ps. 105:19, HCSB)

It was now time for Joseph to reach the place that God had prepared for him. All of his experiences until this point were divinely orchestrated. It seemed like God was playing chess, His every move was working towards one final move. You may not be very happy with your place on the chess board right now. People may be doing vicious things to you. Joseph's brothers meant to harm him, but God used those unpleasant events in Joseph's past to secure the entire family's future. Someone may have tossed you into a pit. Know that this is not your final destination. Look forward to the One who has better things in store for you. His plans for us are not to harm us, but to give us a hope and a future.

The cupbearer then remembered Joseph and spoke to Pharaoh,

> "[12] Now a young Hebrew, a slave of the captain of the guards, was with us there. We told him our dreams, he interpreted our dreams for us, and each had its own interpretation. [13] It turned out just the way he interpreted them to us: I was restored to my position, and the other man was hanged." [14] Then Pharaoh sent for Joseph, and they quickly brought him from the dungeon. He shaved, changed his clothes, and went to Pharaoh." (Gen. 41: 12-14, HCSB)

All this time, it may have seemed to Joseph that God was never going to fulfill his dreams. When the time was right, the 'dreamer' was hastily retrieved from prison and propelled into his destiny. Talk about dreams coming true!

> "For the vision is yet for the appointed time; it testifies about the end and will not lie. Though it delays, wait for it, since it will certainly come and not be late."
> (Hab. 2:3, HCSB)

At just the 'right' time God gave Pharaoh a cryptic dream. Was it a coincidence that the interpreter of dreams was in a prison nearby?

> "[15]Pharaoh said to Joseph, "I have had a dream, and no one can interpret it. But I have heard it said about you that you can hear a dream and interpret it." [16] "I am not able to," Joseph answered Pharaoh. "It is God who will give Pharaoh a favorable answer." (Gen. 41:15-16, HCSB)

Like Daniel, Joseph took the focus off himself and turned it towards God. The egoistical 17-year-old had indeed been refined through his testing. He displayed humility akin to Daniel's. Joseph then gave Pharaoh good counsel to prepare for the famine. His God-given wisdom saved Egypt through the seven years of scarcity.

> "So now, let Pharaoh look for a discerning and wise man and set him over the land of Egypt." (Gen. 41:33, HCSB)

Pharaoh heeded this advice and appointed Joseph the second ruler in Egypt. His exceptional qualities made him the 'man' for the position of power.

> "³⁸ Then Pharaoh said to his servants, "Can we find anyone like this, a man who has God's spirit in him?" ³⁹ So Pharaoh said to Joseph, "Since God has made all this known to you, there is no one as intelligent and wise as you are." (Gen. 41:38-39, HCSB)

This is just like the Babylonians, who acknowledged that Daniel had the Spirit of God upon him. Even Pharaoh could see that Joseph had an exceptional and supernatural Spirit in him.

PROMOTION #3

> "⁴ You will be over my house, and all my people will obey your commands. Only with regard to the throne will I be greater than you." ⁴¹ Pharaoh also said to Joseph, "See, I am placing you over all the land of Egypt." ⁴² Pharaoh removed his signet ring from his hand and put it on Joseph's hand, clothed him with fine linen garments, and placed a gold chain around his neck. ⁴³ He had Joseph ride in his second chariot, and servants called out before him, *"Abrek!"* So he placed him over all the land of Egypt." (Gen. 41:40-43, HCSB)

Joseph seems to receive promotion and gifts just like Daniel. Each one had their fair share of trouble, but each overcame their personal obstacles with flying colors. The excellent Spirit enabled them to ride every tidal wave of adversity. After every test, they receive promotion. By placing Joseph in this place of authority, God preserved Israel and Egypt through the ravaging famine.

SECTION 6

BEARING FRUIT BY THE SPIRIT

FRUITFULNESS

It seems that God's blessing and commission to us is to bear fruit. This is a recurring theme throughout scripture. Fruit brings God glory. It is an outward manifestation of the life of God within.

> "And the second son he named Ephraim, meaning, "God has made me fruitful in the land of my affliction." (Gen. 41:52, HCSB)

> "Joseph is a fruitful vine, a fruitful vine beside a spring; its branches climb over the wall." (Gen. 49:22, HCSB)

Even though Joseph had his roots in Israel, he bore fruit in a foreign environment in spite of adverse conditions. He was rooted and grounded in the ways of his God. In due time, he blossomed and was a source of life to everyone. The persecution he suffered did not destroy him, but God made his arms strong.

> "He is like a tree planted beside streams of water that bears its fruit in season and whose leaf does not wither. Whatever he does prospers." (Ps. 1:3, HCSB)

Throughout the scripture, God's people are compared to a tree or vine. A flourishing Christian bears fruit. For an overall view on fruitfulness, let us go back to Genesis where fruitfulness is first mentioned.

> "⁸The Lord God planted a garden in Eden, in the east, and there He placed the man He had formed. ⁹The Lord God caused to grow out of the ground every tree pleasing in appearance and good for food, including the tree of life in the middle of the garden, as well as the tree of the knowledge of good and evil." (Gen. 2:8-9, HCSB)

> "¹¹Then God said, "Let the earth produce vegetation: seed-bearing plants and fruit trees on the earth bearing fruit with seed in it according to their kinds." And it was so. ¹² The earth produced vegetation: seed-bearing plants according to their kinds and trees bearing fruit with seed in it according to their kinds. And God saw that it was good." (Gen. 1:11-12, HCSB)

We see that the primary purpose of trees is to bear fruit, and God approves of this. He said that it was good. In verse 16, God allowed Adam to eat of the fruit of every tree, all but one. In verse 11, God commanded the earth to bring forth tender vegetation.

GOD'S BLESSING TO ADAM AND EVE

"God blessed them, and God said to them, "Be fruitful, multiply, fill the earth, and subdue it. ..." (Gen. 1:28, HCSB)

God blessed Adam and Eve with the fruit of the womb. God is pro-life.

AFTER THE FALL OF MAN

God cursed the ground.

"[17] And He said to Adam, "Because you listened to your wife's voice and ate from the tree about which I commanded you, 'Do not eat from it': The ground is cursed because of you. You will eat from it by means of painful labor all the days of your life. [18] It will produce thorns and thistles for you, and you will eat the plants of the field."" (Gen. 3:17-18, HCSB)

AFTER THE FLOOD

When Noah offered burnt sacrifices on an altar, the wrath of God was appeased. He brought blessing again upon the earth. It was not as in Eden, but it was an improvement since the fall of man.

"[21] When the Lord smelled the pleasing aroma, He said to Himself, "I will never again curse the ground because of man, even though man's inclination is evil from his youth. And I will never again strike down every living thing as I have done. [22] As long as the earth endures, seed time and harvest, cold and heat, summer and winter, and day and night will not cease." (Gen. 8:21-22, HCSB)

Man still had to toil for his food, but God established the principle of sowing and reaping, seedtime and harvest. He established the seasons.

"God blessed Noah and his sons and said to them, "Be fruitful and multiply and fill the earth." (Gen. 9:1, HCSB)

"Hear this! The days are coming – this is the Lord's declaration – when the plowman will overtake the reaper and the one who treads grapes, the sower of seed. The mountains will drip with sweet wine, and all the hills will flow with it." (Amos 9:13, HCSB)

"²⁶ "The kingdom of God is like this," He said. "A man scatters seed on the ground; ²⁷ he sleeps and rises – night and day, and the seed sprouts and grows – he doesn't know how. ²⁸ The soil produces a crop by itself – first the blade, then the head, and then the ripe grain on the head. ²⁹ But as soon as the crop is ready, he sends for the sickle, because the harvest has come." (Mark 4:26-29, HCSB)

THORNS AND BRIERS

THORNS - A RESULT OF THE CURSE

"Then God said, "Let the earth produce vegetation: seed-bearing plants and fruit trees on the earth bearing fruit with seed in it according to their kinds." (Gen. 1:11, HCSB)

Before the fall of man, the tender trees brought fruit on their own. There was no toil on man's part. The blessing of God brought tender vegetation and fruit. After the fall, the ground was cursed and it bore thorns and thistles.

"¹⁷…The ground is cursed because of you. You will eat from it by means of painful labor all the days of your life. ¹⁸ It will produce thorns and thistles for you, and you will eat the plants of the field." (Gen. 3:17-18, HCSB)

Thorns and thistles are plants without fruit. A thistle is a luxuriantly growing but useless plant. After the curse man would get fruit only through hard labor.

THE VINEYARD OF THE SLOTHFUL

"³⁰ I went by the field of a slacker and by the vineyard of a man lacking sense. ³¹ Thistles had come up everywhere, weeds covered the ground, and the stone wall was ruined. ³² I saw, and took it to heart; I looked, and received instruction: ³³ a little sleep, a little slumber, a little folding of the arms to rest, ³⁴ and your poverty will come like a robber, your need, like a bandit." (Pro. 24:30-34, HCSB)

Spiritual slothfulness leads to spiritual poverty. It will not be long before a slothful man's spiritual state manifests in the physical realm. The result will be some kind of physical poverty. This does not imply that just a man's riches will be lost, but it means that any area of his life may lack the prosperity and success that can only come from God's blessing on the life of a man whose heart prospers.

ISRAEL – GOD'S VINEYARD

"¹I will sing about the one I love, a song about my loved one's vineyard: The one I love had a vineyard on a very fertile hill. ² He broke up the soil, cleared it of stones, and planted it with the finest vines. He built a tower in the middle of it and even dug out a winepress there. He expected it to yield good grapes, but it yielded worthless grapes. ³So now, residents of Jerusalem and men of Judah, please judge between Me and My vineyard. ⁴ What more could I have done for My vineyard than I did? Why, when I expected a yield of good grapes, did it yield worthless grapes?⁵ Now I will tell you what I am about to do to My vineyard: I will remove its hedge, and it will be consumed; I will tear down its wall, and it will be trampled. ⁶I will make it a wasteland. It will not be pruned or weeded; thorns and briers will grow up. I will also give orders to the clouds that rain should not fall on it. ⁷For the vineyard of the Lord of Hosts is the house of Israel, and the men of Judah, the plant He delighted in. He looked for justice but saw injustice, for righteousness, but heard cries of wretchedness." (Isa. 5:1-7, HCSB)

God compares idolatrous Israel to a vineyard on a very fruitful hill. In verses 4 and 5, God has tended it and given it the best, but it yielded wild grapes. Its walls and hedges will be broken and the city will be laid to waste. When God was expecting to find the fruit of righteousness and judgement in Israel, He found instead the wild fruit of oppression and the cry of the oppressed.

In Isaiah 7, Judah is in a state of spiritual decline under the reign of King Ahaz. This is the King Ahaz that made another altar to replace the bronze altar of the Temple. He rearranged the furniture of the temple and even shut the doors of the temple.

Israel was in a state of moral decline, as it was deep in the practice of idolatry. God was saying that they were not spiritually bearing fruit. Israel would be this vineyard that would be desolate and given over to bearing thorns and briers.

> "And on that day every place where there were 1,000 vines, worth 1,000 pieces of silver, will become thorns and briers. (Isa. 7:23, HCSB)

This came to pass when both Israel and Judah were sent into captivity. Israel was dispersed in Assyria. Judah's walls were broken down and the city burnt to the ground.

FRUIT OR THORNS – BLESSING OR CURSE

> "⁷For ground that has drunk the rain that has often fallen on it and that produces vegetation useful to those it is cultivated for receives a blessing from God. ⁸ But if it produces thorns and thistles, it is worthless and about to be cursed, and will be burned at the end." (Heb. 6:7-8, HCSB)

It is plain to see that the land which bears fruit is blessed, and the land that yields thorns will be cursed. We must desire to be the land that drinks in the rain of the Holy Ghost and so bears the fruit of the Spirit. Blessings will then flow into every part of our life.

JESUS WORE THE CROWN OF THORNS

> "They twisted together a crown of thorns, put it on His head, and placed a reed in His right hand. And they knelt down before Him and mocked Him: "Hail, King of the Jews!" (Matt. 27:29, HCSB)

Jesus took the symbol of the curse and affliction and wore it as His crown. He was cursed so that we may be blessed.

> "Abraham looked up and saw a ram caught in the thicket by its horns. So Abraham went and took the ram and offered it as a burnt offering in place of his son." (Gen. 22:13, HCSB)

Jesus is the ram caught in the thicket, which became the substitute for Isaac. Jesus died in our place so that we might live for Him. The ram's horns were caught in the thorns. Jesus' head was in the thorny crown. Does this seem like a coincidence?

THE WILDERNESS FLOURISHES

> "¹³...for the ground of my people growing thorns and briers, indeed, for every joyous house in the joyful city. ¹⁴ For the palace will be forsaken, the busy city abandoned. The hill and the watchtower will become barren places forever, the joy of wild donkeys, and a pasture for flocks..." (Isa. 32: 13-14, HCSB)

Isaiah 32:9-14 portray a picture of desolation.

> "⁹Stand up, you complacent women; listen to me. Pay attention to what I say, you overconfident daughters.¹⁰ In a little more than a year you overconfident ones will shudder, for the vintage will fail and the harvest will not come. ¹¹ Shudder, you complacent ones; tremble, you overconfident ones! Strip yourselves bare and put sackcloth around your waists." (Isa. 32: 9-11, HCSB)

As can be seen from these verses, God rebuked His people for being at ease. They were not fervently seeking His face as they should. They had become spiritually slothful, which resulted in physical thorns and briers in their land.

> "¹⁵ ...until the Spirit from heaven is poured out on us. Then the desert will become an orchard, and the orchard will seem like a forest. ¹⁶ Then justice will inhabit the wilderness, and righteousness will dwell in the orchard. ¹⁷ The result of righteousness will be peace; the effect of righteousness will be quiet confidence forever. ¹⁸ Then my people will dwell in a peaceful place, in safe and secure dwellings." (Isa. 32:15-18, HCSB)

From Isaiah 32:15 onwards, the scenery transforms from barrenness to fruitfulness. What brings about the change? Change transpires after the outpouring of the Holy Spirit.

The outpouring of the Holy Spirit on our lives will cause us to bear fruit as we should. We will be the fruitful 'land' that receives the blessing of God. When His righteousness flows through us, our lives will bear the fruit of peace and safety. Justice and righteousness are followed by peace and safety.

Does your life lack peace and safety? Seek an outpouring of the Spirit. He can bring righteousness, safety, peace, joy and wholeness to our lives. We may experience the lack of these blessings from time to time, but God does not want us to remain that way forever. His desire is for us to have these basic blessings. It will all be found in seeking His face.

THORNS AND BRIERS REPLACED

"[10] For just as rain and snow fall from heaven and do not return there without saturating the earth and making it germinate and sprout, and providing seed to sow and food to eat, [11]so My word that comes from My mouth will not return to Me empty, but it will accomplish what I please and will prosper in what I send it to do." [12]You will indeed go out with joy and be peacefully guided; the mountains and the hills will break into singing before you, and all the trees of the field will clap their hands. [13]Instead of the thorn bush, a cypress will come up, and instead of the brier, a myrtle will come up; it will make a name for Yahweh as an everlasting sign that will not be destroyed." (Isa. 55:10-13, HCSB)

God wants His children to be in peace and go forth with joy. His word to us is a seed sown on the ground with the potential to become a fruit bearing plant. Unless it rains, there will be no harvest. Pray for the outpouring of the Spirit to bring His word to pass. The rain of the Spirit will take away the thorns and briers in our lives and replace them with the fruit of wholeness. How we need the rain of the Spirit! Let it rain!

FRUIT FOR GLORY

"My Father is glorified by this: that you produce much fruit and prove to be My disciples." (John 15:8, HCSB)

FRUITLESS FIG TREE #1

"¹³ After seeing in the distance a fig tree with leaves, He went to find out if there was anything on it. When He came to it, He found nothing but leaves, because it was not the season for figs. ¹⁴ He said to it, "May no one ever eat fruit from you again!" And His disciples heard it." (Mark 11:13-14, HCSB)

"Early in the morning, as they were passing by, they saw the fig tree withered from the roots up." (Mark 11:20, HCSB)

There are two seasons for figs – the early season and the late one. It is during this early season that Jesus came to the tree. Usually the leaves sprout at the same time as the figs, so Jesus expected to find fruit on this tree rich in foliage. From this passage, it is clear that Jesus takes 'fruit' very seriously.

FRUITLESS FIG TREE #2

"⁶ And He told this parable: A man had a fig tree that was planted in his vineyard. He came looking for fruit on it and found none. ⁷ He told the vineyard worker, 'Listen, for three years I have come looking for fruit on this fig tree and haven't found any. Cut it down! Why should it even waste the soil?' ⁸ "But he replied to him, 'Sir, leave it this year also, until I dig around it and fertilize it. ⁹ Perhaps it will bear fruit next year, but if not, you can cut it down.'"" (Luke 13:6-9, HCSB)

In both these stories people come to the tree expecting to find fruit on it. This is because a tree's primary purpose is to bear fruit. A tree is destined to bear fruit. It is the very purpose for its existence. The Holy Spirit is the dresser in this parable. Allow Him to dig into your hearts and fertilize it. He alone can turn barrenness into fruitfulness. Jesus is the Vine; we are the branches. The Holy Spirit is like the life that flows from the vine to the branches.

PARABLE OF THE SOWER

This parable has four types of ground, all of which receive the same seed. The sower desires for each seed to go down deep into the soil and grow into a mature plant that bears fruit.

GROUND #1

The seeds did not even make it into the soil, as they fell by the wayside and the birds ate them. This is a parallel to the word barely penetrating the heart of man, then the devil steals it away.

GROUND #2

The seeds could not go deep enough into the shallow soil. The sun scorched the saplings and they withered away. These are like people who do not allow the word to take root and shrivel up in the persecution that comes.

GROUND #3

> "Other seed fell among thorns, and the thorns came up and choked it, and it didn't produce a crop." (Mark 4:7, HCSB)

> "As for the seed that fell among thorns, these are the ones who, when they have heard, go on their way and are choked with worries, riches, and pleasures of life, and produce no mature fruit." (Luke 8:14, HCSB)

These are people who gladly receive the word, but they relish the things of this world more than the word - the worries and pleasures of this life, the lust of the eyes, the lust of the flesh and the pride of life choke out the word, making them unfruitful.

GROUND #4

> "Still others fell on good ground and produced a crop that increased 30, 60, and 100 times what was sown." (Mark 4: 8, HCSB)

> "But the seed in the good ground — these are the ones who, having heard the word with an honest and good heart, hold on to it and by enduring, bear fruit." (Luke 8:15, HCSB)

From this passage, we infer that the seed is the word and that the ground is our heart. The same seed falls on our hearts. How far we allow it to penetrate determines our harvest. Those whose hearts are the 'good' ground ensure to hear the word and absorb it. By not allowing the riches, cares, and pleasures of this life to interfere, they allow the word to penetrate and permeate. They bear fruit. Different people have different yields of 0%, 30%, 60%, or 100%. There are different levels of fruit-bearing. The amount of fruit we yield is proportionate to the amount of the word we allow to soak into our heart's ground.

ABUNDANT FRUIT

> "Israel is a lush vine; it yields fruit for itself. The more his fruit increased, the more he increased the altars. The better his land produced, the better they made the sacred pillars." (Hos. 10:1, HCSB)

In Hosea 10, we see that prosperous Israel has gone into idolatry. They worshipped the calves of Samaria, the Baals of Assyria, and erected multiple altars to idols. Hosea was prophesying about the result of this idol worship and departing from God. God had blessed them. This spiritual blessing also flowed into the material realm. After a while, Israel started producing fruit for itself and not for Jehovah. Israel was getting rich and fat of the good fruit of the promised land, but was not producing the desired fruit. Spiritual decline results in 'thorns and thistles'.

> "The high places of Aven, the sin of Israel, will be destroyed; thorns and thistles will grow over their altars…" (Hos. 10:8, HCSB)

It is not enough to just bear some fruit. Here Israel got complacent at its level of fruit bearing and began to bear fruit for selfish reasons. Jesus said in John 15:8 that we bear much fruit – for God's glory. God called Israel to repent.

> "Sow righteousness for yourselves and reap faithful love; break up your unplowed ground. It is time to seek the Lord until He comes and sends righteousness on you like the rain. (Hos. 10:12, HCSB)

SPIRITUAL FAT

SIN OF SODOM

> "⁴⁹Now this was the iniquity of your sister Sodom: she and her daughters had pride, plenty of food, and comfortable security, but didn't support the poor and needy. ⁵⁰They were haughty and did detestable things before Me, so I removed them when I saw this." (Ezek. 16:49-50, HCSB)

We may reach a stage in life when we bear fruit, which is good. We cannot remain at that level forever, because there is a danger of getting complacent and spiritually fat. Sodom's sin was not just sodomy. That was just one of the outcomes of an isolated prosperous life. They had forgotten to help and identify with the poor and needy, and over time arrogance, fullness of bread, and idleness became a lifestyle. This complacent lifestyle gave room for the sin of Sodomy for which they were destroyed.

Our fruit is meant to abound. What do you do with an abundance of fruit? Eat it all? No, we are meant to share it for God's glory. We can't just hog the wealth for ourselves. It is just not healthy.

JESHURUN

"¹²The Lord alone led him, with no help from a foreign god. ¹³ He made him ride on the heights of the land and eat the produce of the field. He nourished him with honey from the rock and oil from flint-like rock, ¹⁴ cream from the herd and milk from the flock, with the fat of lambs, rams from Bashan, and goats, with the choicest grains of wheat; you drank wine from the finest grapes. ¹⁵ Then Jeshurun became fat and rebelled – you became fat, bloated, and gorged. He abandoned the God who made him and scorned the Rock of his salvation."
(Deut. 32:12-15, HCSB)

Jeshurun (another name for Israel) was fruitful and increased. The blessing of God made him rich. He grew obese and kicked back against God. We are meant to be a conduit of the life of God. His life will flow through us to the needy. If we hog all His goodness for ourselves, our pipes become clogged and we get swollen. Like Jeshurun, we may be in danger of developing calloused, thick skin. This is not meant to be. He slowly turned and forsook his God. This process of drifting is slow and difficult to notice. May we never lightly esteem Jehovah!

NEBUCHADNEZZAR

"I, Nebuchadnezzar was at ease in my house, and flourishing in my palace."
(Dan. 4:4, HCSB)

Nebuchadnezzar had a dream.

"¹⁰ In the visions of my mind as I was lying in bed, I saw this: There was a tree in the middle of the earth, and its height was great. ¹¹The tree grew large and strong; its top reached to the sky, and it was visible to the ends of the earth. ¹² Its leaves were beautiful, its fruit was abundant, and on it was food for all. Wild animals found shelter under it, the birds of the air lived in its branches, and every creature was fed from it." (Dan. 4: 10-12, HCSB)

The tree was later cut down and only the stump left. This was a warning of things to come for Nebuchadnezzar. Notice that he was a fruitful tree. He was a great king, who conquered and had dominion over the major kingdoms of the earth. This was his destiny and purpose. It is God who gave him the kingdoms of the earth. After a while the prosperity got to his head, and he took the glory for himself.

"…that tree is you, the king. For you have become great and strong: your greatness has grown and even reaches the sky, and your dominion extends to the ends of the earth." (Dan. 4:22, HCSB)

Daniel gave him the key to preventing his downfall..

> "Therefore, may my advice seem good to you my king. Separate yourself from your sins by doing what is right, and from your injustices by showing mercy to the needy. Perhaps there will be an extension of your prosperity." (Dan. 4:27, HCSB)

A year later this incident had faded from Nebuchadnezzar's mind.

> "The king exclaimed, "Is this not Babylon the Great that I have built by **my** vast power to be a royal residence and to display **my** majestic glory?" (Dan. 4:30, HCSB)

Nebuchadnezzar's power, might, majesty and kingdom were given to him by God. Notice how he attributes his power, glory, and success to himself. The flourishing king was swollen with pride. As Daniel predicted, he was cast out of his kingdom, stripped of his glory and had to live like a wild beast for seven years.

> "But at the end of those days, I, Nebuchadnezzar, looked up to heaven, and my sanity returned to me. Then I praised the Most High and honored and glorified Him who lives forever: For His dominion is an everlasting dominion and His kingdom is from generation to generation." (Dan. 4:34, HCSB)

Nebuchadnezzar gave God honor and glory and then he is restored. He acknowledged and honored the King of Kings, and became a 'fruitful tree' once more.

This is a repetition of prideful Lucifer being cut down to the ground, and tossed out like a worthless branch. Let them be an example to us of how hubris can hinder the fruit!

EPHRAIM

God referred to Israel as his son 'Ephraim', a name of endearment. In the book of Hosea, Ephraim had joined himself to idols, engaging in spiritual adultery. A spirit of prostitution led them astray from the living God and affected their fruitfulness. In Hosea 9, God recalled the times when He saw Israel like grapes in the wilderness and like the first fruit of a fig tree. As time progressed, Israel forgot His Maker and erected temples to idols and Baals. Their glory would flee away as a bird, and they would be bereaved of their offspring. There would be no birth, gestation, and no conception. They would have miscarrying wombs and dry breasts. Even if they raised children, they would be bereaved. Their spiritual lack of fruit would manifest in the physical.

> "Ephraim is smitten, their root is dried up, they shall bear **no fruit**: yea, though they bring forth, yet will I slay even the beloved fruit of their womb." (Hos. 9:16, KJV)

Do you feel as though there are areas in your life that are unfruitful? It just may be that you may need to look inward, cleave to the Vine, and start bearing fruit for God. Only when Israel turned back to God was it healed. Just as Hosea bought adulterous Gomer to be his wife, God would bring adulterous Israel back to Himself. Jehovah would heal Israel's fickle heart and cause it to flourish again.

> "Ephraim, why should I have anything more to do with idols? It is I who answer and watch over him. I am like a flourishing pine tree; **your fruit comes from Me.**"
> (Hos. 14:8, HCSB)

God tells Israel that He is not like the idols. He is as the evergreen tree, full of life. He is the source of our fruitfulness. Without Him, we can do nothing. Unless we abide in the Vine, we will not bear the abundant fruit that He desires

FRUIT THAT REMAINS

"You did not choose Me, but I chose you. I appointed you that you should go out and produce fruit and that your fruit should remain, so that whatever you ask the Father in My name, He will give you." (John 15:16, HCSB)

In the parable of the sower, we saw that the four types of ground had four types of yield – 0, 30, 60 and 100-fold.

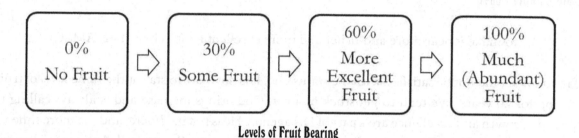

Levels of Fruit Bearing

LEVELS OF FRUIT BEARING

Each ground (heart) received the same seed (Word), scattered by the same sower. The harvest was determined by the way they received and responded to the seed. In John 15, we encounter the same four categories of fruit-bearing.

1. NO FRUIT - 0%

"Every branch in Me that does not produce fruit He removes..." (John 15:2, HCSB)

Here the word 'removes' means to raise up, elevate, lift up, or to take and apply to any use. This refers to a vine that does not bear fruit and is lying on the ground, most likely being trodden under. The vinedresser carefully raises up the branch, washes it, and secures it to the trellis. Jesus does not cut us off from His love, but beckons us with a higher calling to bear fruit.

2. SOME FRUIT - 30%

"...and He prunes every branch that produces fruit so that it will produce more fruit." (John 15:2, HCSB)

The Greek word for 'prune' also means to cleanse of filth or impurity; to prune trees and vines from useless shoots. It can also be a metaphor meaning to cleanse or expiate from guilt. Verse 3 says that Jesus has cleansed the branches by His word and teaching. It is His word that washes us from the dust of this world. This reminds me of the time when Jesus washed the disciples' feet.

"⁵Next, He poured water into a basin and began to wash His disciples' feet and to dry them with the towel tied around Him." (John 13:5, HCSB)

""You will never wash my feet – ever!" Peter said. Jesus replied, "If I don't wash you, you have no part with Me."" (John 13:8, HCSB)

In the parable of the sower, the cares, riches and pleasures of this life keep the plant from bearing fruit. The only antidote for these very real-life distractions is being washed in His Word daily. It will cleanse us so that we might bear fruit for His glory.

3. MORE FRUIT - 60%

"...to make it bear more and richer and more excellent fruit." (John 15:2, AMPC)

Christians should not be satisfied with the status quo. It is not okay to stay at the same level of fruit-bearing for 20 years. We tend to get stuck in a rut. God brings increase and is always calling us upward. Growth and excellence are a part of His agenda. He is not mediocre, and the more time we spend with Him, the more His excellence should rub off onto us. We are called to bear richer and more excellent fruit. This is similar to the passage about going from glory to glory and strength to strength. The only one who can tell you how much you have grown is you. Only you really know if you are increasing or becoming dormant. The Holy Spirit will reveal to us our state of growth and fruit production if we ask Him.

4. ABUNDANT FRUIT - 100%

"I am the vine; you are the branches. The one who remains in Me and I in him produces much fruit, because you can do nothing without Me." (John 15:5, HCSB)

In order to bear abundant fruit, we need to abide in Jesus. We understand the Vine is Jesus, the Vinedresser is the Father; and the branches are the Children of God. Apart from Jesus, we can do nothing.

ABIDE

The word 'abide' in itself means to remain; to be vitally united, sojourn, tarry, last, endure, continue to be present, not to perish, and not to depart. It can be in reference to place, time, state or condition. When we bear abundant fruit, John 15:8 says, "My Father is glorified by this: that you produce much fruit and prove to be My disciples".

"If anyone does not remain in Me, he is thrown aside like a branch and he withers. They gather them, throw them into the fire, and they are burned." (John 15:6, HCSB)

This does not mean that such a branch will be thrown into hellfire. Jesus is just showing how useless a fruitless branch is.

> "⁹As the Father has loved Me; I have also loved you. Remain in My love. ¹⁰ If you keep My commands you will remain in My love, just as I have kept My Father's commands and remain in His love." (John 15:9-10, HCSB)

We can abide by the words of John 15:9 and 10 of remaining in His love and by obeying His commands. This is done by staying in constant communion and by abiding in His Word. What does the Holy Spirit have to do with abiding in the Vine?

> "But the anointing which ye have received of Him abideth in you, and ye need not that any man teach you: but as the same anointing teacheth you of all things, and is truth, and is no lie, and even as it hath taught you, ye shall **abide** in Him." (1 John 2:27, KJV)

The Holy Ghost is the 'anointing' believers receive. He is the One who will guide us into all truth.

He reveals Jesus to us. Listening to the Spirit speaking to the churches helps us stay connected to the Vine. The Spirit is the life that flows from the Vine to the branches.

FRUIT OF THE SPIRIT

"But the fruit of the Spirit is..." (Gal. 5:22, HCSB)

Whenever a verse begins with 'But', one must study the verse preceding it to properly understand the second verse. Before studying the 'Fruit of the Spirit', it would help to study the opposing 'Works of the Flesh'.

WORKS OF THE FLESH

"[19] Now the works of the flesh are obvious: sexual immorality, moral impurity, promiscuity, [20] idolatry, sorcery, hatreds, strife, jealousy, outbursts of anger, selfish ambitions, dissensions, factions, [21] envy, drunkenness, carousing, and anything similar. I tell you about these things in advance – as I told you before – that those who practice such things will not inherit the kingdom of God." (Gal. 5:19-21, HCSB)

From personal experience, just skimming through these verses in the past seemed like a blur of archaic words! On a closer inspection, some of these traits are very close to home. Lots of these behavioral tendencies are very natural. Some of them look worse than others, but they are all classified together. If we threw a person that exhibited one trait into a prison cell, the adulterer and idolater would be incarcerated along with the angry and the envious. We tend to think some sins are worse than others. Those who bow down to an idol or commit fornication are as bad as the very spiritual people who create factions in church. Maybe the impact of some sins are worse than others, but they are all sin. The conclusion is that we all need help!

The fruit of the Spirit is the opposite of all these works of the flesh. Only when we realize that we possess some of these tendencies will we more fully understand the need we have for the fullness of the Spirit. Only the Holy Spirit can root out these ungodly traits and cause us to bear the fruit of the Spirit.

FOUR SINS OF LUST

The four sins of lust are adultery, fornication, uncleanness, and lasciviousness.

1. Adultery: Marriage covenants are broken. Unlawful sexual relations between a man and woman, where both or either is married

2. Fornication: Illicit sexual relations outside the marriage covenant; selling oneself for lust

3. Uncleanness: Opposite of purity; sexual perversion (sodomy, lesbianism, homosexuality, etc.)

4. Lasciviousness: This can imply licentiousness, lewdness, lustfulness, and unchastely behavior; Partaking of or promoting lewd emotions, anything tending to foster sex, sin, and lust

TWO SINS OF IMPIETY OR SUPERSTITION

The two sins of impiety or superstition are idolatry and witchcraft.

1. Idolatry: Image worship; anything on which the affections are passionately set; extravagant admiration of the heart

2. Witchcraft: Sorcery; practice of dealing with evil spirits; using spells, charms, or drugs to inflict pain, death, or to bring health, love, and blessings

NINE SINS OF TEMPER

The nine sins of temper are hatred, variance, emulations, wrath, strife, seditions, heresies, envying, and murder.

1. Hatred: Bitter dislike; abhorrence, malice; ill-will against anyone; tendency to hold grudges against or to be angry at someone

2. Variance: Dissensions, discord; quarrels; debates; disputes

3. Emulations: Envies, jealousies; striving to excel at the expense of another; seeking to surpass or outdo others with unkind intentions

4. Wrath: Indignation and fierceness; turbulent passions; domestic and civil turmoil; rage; determined and lasting anger

5. Strife: Disputations, strife about words; angry contentions; contest for superiority or advantage; strenuous endeavor to payback in kind the wrongs done to one

6. Seditions: Divisions; parties and factions; stirring up strife in religion, government, homes etc. For example, Dathan and Abiram formed a faction against Moses

7. Heresies: A sect; a doctrinal view that is at variance with the recognized tenets of a system or church. For example, a sect came up in the early church demanding that all believers had to be circumcised. They were trying to dilute the freedom that Christ had given

8. Envying: Pain, ill-will and jealousy at the good fortune or blessing of another; the basest of all degrading passions. For example, Saul envied David. It became the root of all his ill-will against David

9. Murder: To kill; hatred towards anyone

TWO SINS OF APPETITE

The two sins of appetite are drunkenness and revelings.

1. Drunkenness: Living intoxicated; a slave to drink

2. Revelings: Lascivious and boisterous feastings with obscene music; carousings

What is the cure for this wretchedness? Who shall deliver us from this body of sin, with all its depraved tendencies? The answer lies in Galatians 5:16.

> "I say then, walk by the Spirit and you will not carry out the desire of the flesh."
> (Gal. 5:16, HCSB)

Here are two extremes. Either we walk in the Spirit and bear the fruit of the Spirit, or we will heed the commands of the sinful nature.

> "[22]But the fruit of the Spirit is love, joy, peace, patience, kindness, goodness, faith, [23]gentleness, self-control. Against such things there is no law." (Gal. 5:22-23, HCSB)

Remember that all these characteristics were seen in Jesus, as He was full of the Spirit of God. The fruit is the work that the Holy Spirit's presence accomplishes in our lives. We need to stay connected to the Vine, and allow the 'sap' of the Holy Ghost to flow through us so we will bear fruit.

NINE-FOLD FRUIT OF THE SPIRIT

God's love is poignantly described in 1 Corinthians 13. The nine-fold fruit of the spirit are love, joy, peace, long suffering, gentleness, goodness, faith, meekness, and temperance.

1. Love (Agape): Divine love; a strong, ardent, tender devotion to the well-being of someone

2. Joy: Gladness

3. Peace: The state of quietness and rest, harmony, order, and security in the midst of turmoil and distress

4. Long suffering: Patient endurance; to bear long with others without murmuring or resentment

5. Gentleness: Benignity; kindness

6. Goodness: Uprightness of heart and life

7. Faith: Belief

8. Meekness: Not weakness; is separate from gentleness; balanced in tempers and passions. The word 'meekness' is related to horses. Only a meek horse would take the bit. It may have been a strong horse, but only a willing horse would submit to a bit. Once a horse took to the bit, the horse and rider moved as one entity. Meekness has also been described as 'great power under restraint'. Jesus was meek. He had the power to summon a legion of angels to save Himself, but He had the strength (meekness) to submit to God's plan of suffering at the hands of men

9. Temperance: Self-control (the virtue of one who masters his desires and passions, especially his sensual appetites); moderation in the indulgence of the appetites and passions

""Everything is permissible for me," but not everything is helpful. "Everything is permissible for me," but I will not be brought under the control of anything." (1 Cor. 6:12, HCSB)

SECTION 7
WALKING IN THE SPIRIT

SPIRIT, SOUL, AND BODY

"Now may the God of peace Himself sanctify you completely. And may your **spirit, soul, and body** be kept sound and blameless for the coming of our Lord Jesus Christ." (1 Thess. 5:23, HCSB)

Man is made up of three parts. We are a spirit, we have a soul, and we live in a body.

1. The human spirit (*pneuma*) - Our innermost being, also called the heart. This part of us will never die, but in eternity will remain in eternal life or death. This is the part of us that communes with God, the place where God is enthroned as king.

2. The soul (*psyche*) - The mind, will and emotions. Our soul makes us a distinct personality.

3. The body (*soma*) - The temporary habitation for our spirit. It is guided by the five senses of sight, touch, taste, sound, and smell. Our body is dust that returns to dust when we die.

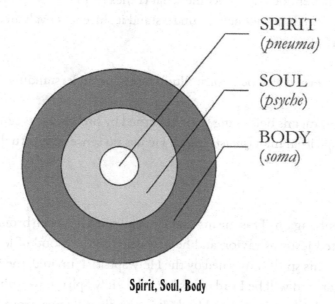

SPIRIT
(*pneuma*)

SOUL
(*psyche*)

BODY
(*soma*)

Spirit, Soul, Body

When God created Adam, He breathed the breath of life into the body of clay and Adam became a living being. Adam's spirit was born of God's Spirit. When Adam sinned, his spirit died instantly.

A spiritual death is separation from God. Death began to work from the inside out, and his body started to decay slowly. All humans are born with a dead spirit. We are all born as slaves to sin. This is why God sent Jesus to reconcile the estranged human race back to Him.

"So it is written: The first man Adam became a living being; the last Adam became a life-giving Spirit." (1 Cor. 15: 45, HCSB)

When a person accepts Jesus as Lord and believes and confesses His death and resurrection, God makes the dead spirit come alive. This person is now a child of God and walks in a relationship with God, just as Adam did. The spirit is born-again. The person now has eternal life. Jesus is the firstborn from the dead. As He lives, we shall live also. He is resurrected with a glorified body. Death has no claim over Him. Death has lost its sting.

We too await the redemption of the body at His appearing in the clouds when we will be transformed in a twinkling of an eye. Until that time, believers experience death of their natural bodies. During the rapture, these that are asleep will be raised first in a glorified body.

"For as in Adam all die, so also in Christ all will be made alive." (1 Cor. 15:22, HCSB)

THE NATURAL MAN

This man is not connected to God at all, but is driven by his fleshly nature. His soul is influenced by his five senses, and his spirit is dead. This is why he cannot discern spiritual things. After Adam fell, his spirit died and Adam became a natural man.

"But the unbeliever does not welcome what comes from God's Spirit, because it is foolishness to him; he is not able to understand it since it is evaluated spiritually." (1 Cor. 2:14, HCSB)

Spiritual things are discerned as God's Spirit illuminates our understanding.

Natural man (*psychikos*) means belonging to or governed by breath. He is sensual and is an animal man as opposed to a spiritual man (*pnuematikos*). He has no sense of spiritual values.

THE SPIRITUAL MAN

The spiritual man is born again. This means that his dead spirit has been brought to life by the Holy Spirit when he accepted Jesus as savior, and he is washed in the blood of Jesus. He is now a new man who can be led by his spirit (governed by the Holy Spirit). If invited, the Holy Spirit will reside within the spirit of man and will be Lord of his life. The Holy Spirit now influences the born-again believer's spirit, which directs his soul and flesh. It is a godly influence from the inside out. This is how He changes us from the inside.

"The spiritual person, however, can evaluate everything, yet he himself cannot be evaluated by anyone." (1 Cor. 2:15, HCSB)

The Spiritual Man (*pneumatikos*) implies one living under the control of the Holy Spirit; he has the mind of Christ; minds the things of the Spirit; he esteems spiritual things above the sensual; is a new creation in Christ.

THE CARNAL MAN

This man is one who is born-again but is not submitted to the Lordship of Christ. He would rather let his flesh rule and call the shots. The negative influence flows in the wrong direction. He responds to his five senses, his soul enjoys it, and his spirit is not the dominant part of his being as it should be. This is why some believers act worse than those who do not know God.

There is an ongoing battle between our spirit and our flesh. With our hearts, we long after God, but our flesh pulls us towards earthly things. Even Paul was caught in this terrible battle. It is when we press on and seek God that we will be victorious. If we give in to the demands of the flesh, we will become carnal and act as mere men.

Today is the day that you can put an end to this carnal rule in your life. Paul cries out for an answer, and he thanks God that he will be saved from this battle through our Lord Jesus Christ. We should not just call Him 'Lord', but really and truly hand over the reins of our life to Christ.

> "Brothers, I was not able to speak to you as spiritual people but as people of the flesh, as babies in Christ." (1 Cor. 3:1, HCSB)

Carnal Man (*sarkikos*) indicates fleshly (derived from the Greek word *sarks* meaning flesh) dominance, governed by mere human nature not by the Spirit of God.

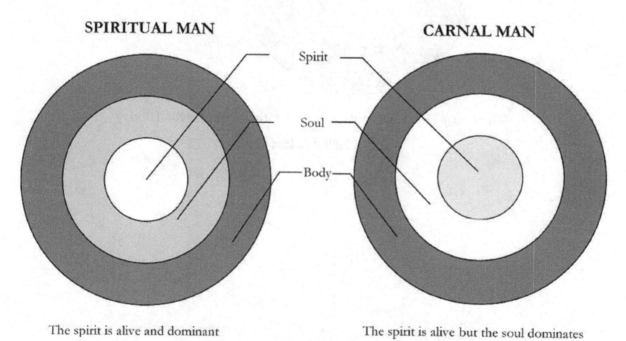

SPIRITUAL MAN   **CARNAL MAN**

Spirit — Soul — Body

The spirit is alive and dominant   The spirit is alive but the soul dominates

Spiritual and Carnal Man

"²² For in my inner self I joyfully agree with God's law. ²³ But I see a different law in the parts of my body, waging war against the law of my mind and taking me prisoner to the law of sin in the parts of my body." (Rom. 7:22-23, HCSB)

The Law of Sin is at work in the flesh and is trying to dominate. The Law of Reason is at work in the mind. The Battle is over the soul. The Flesh pulls on our mind, will, and emotions and tries to pull us away from spiritual things and make us more worldly. When we give in to the pull of the flesh, we become carnal Christians who are babes in Christ.

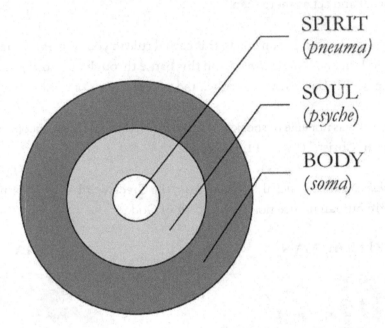

SPIRIT
(*pneuma*)

SOUL
(*psyche*)

BODY
(*soma*)

The Law of Reason (Soul) is at war with the Law of Sin (Body)

Battle of the Laws

"I say then, walk by the Spirit and you will not carry out the desire of the flesh." (Gal. 5:16, HCSB)

The word 'fulfill' means to carry out the aspects of a command. There are two extremes – we are either walking in the Spirit, or we are heeding the commands of the sinful nature.

"For if you live according to [the dictates of] the flesh, **you will surely die**. But if through the power of the [Holy] Spirit you are [habitually] putting to death (making extinct, deadening) the [evil] deeds prompted by the body, you shall [really and genuinely] **live forever**." (Rom. 8: 12-13, AMPC)

Does the phrase "You will surely die …" sound familiar? Here is a parallel in scripture, when Adam and Eve had a similar scenario before them in Eden.

"…but you must not eat from the tree of the knowledge of good and evil, for on the day you eat from it, **you will certainly die**." (Gen. 2:17, HCSB)

When God told Adam and Eve not to eat from the Tree of Knowledge, He was not giving them a choice, but a directive. He did not give them the option of eating either from the Tree of Life or the Tree of Knowledge. God specifically commanded them not to eat of the Tree of Knowledge, because he did not want them to experience evil and the misery that came along with it. However, Adam made the choice to disobey God. Let us not do the same in following the dictates of the flesh. If we live in the Spirit, we will enjoy the fullness of life.

If you live according to the flesh, you will surely die.

But if by the Spirit you put to death the deeds of the body, you will live.

Romans 8:13

Two Trees

> "In fact, God knows that when you eat it your eyes will be opened and you will be like God, knowing good and evil." (Gen. 3:5, HCSB)

The Hebrew word *yada* means know, perceive and see, find out and discern, discriminate, distinguish, or know by experience.

Adam and Eve already knew the concept of good, as God had created everything to the best of its nature. They were living the good life. Evil existed, and God knew of it, but everything about Him is good. There is no evil in Him. God meant for them to experience His goodness and not know and experience sin and the misery acquainted with it. If they ate of the Tree of Knowledge they would know good and evil, but if they ate of the Tree of Life they would know Life eternal.

Have you ever wondered what eternal life really is? It does imply that you will live forever, but to what purpose? Those who are in Hell do continue to exist, but are in Eternal Death (separation from God). So, what then is Eternal Life? Is it just a mere existence in heaven forever? The answer to that is in John 17.

> "This is eternal life: that they may know You, the only true God, and the One You have sent – Jesus Christ." (John 17:3, HCSB)

The word 'know' here is *ginosko* which means to learn or come to know, get a knowledge of, to feel; perceive, to understand; to become acquainted with. It is also a Jewish term for intimate relations between a man and a woman. It implies a deeper, intimate understanding of a person or thing.

We shall dwell with God in eternity and fully know Him and walk in perfect undisrupted communion with Him. We will have true Life only when we are one with God. We have an important choice set before us today. We can choose carnality and know (*yada*) the evil that comes with sin, or we can choose Eternal Life, and know (*ginosko*) the only true God and Jesus.

THE PATH OF TEMPTATION

EVE'S DECEPTION AND FALL INTO TEMPTATION

There is a pattern of temptation that the devil went through when he tempted Adam and Eve. He uses the same pattern to tempt believers today. The enemy's strategy has not changed since Eden.

> "Now the serpent was the most cunning of all the wild animals that the Lord God had made. He said to the woman, "Did God really say, 'You can't eat from any tree in the garden'?"" (Gen. 3:1, HCSB)

1.   Satan challenges God's word and causes us to doubt it.

     ""No! You will not die," the serpent said to the woman." (Gen. 3:4, HCSB)

2.   He contradicts God's word. God said that they would 'surely' die.

     "In fact, God knows that when you eat it your eyes will be opened and you will be like God, knowing good and evil." (Gen. 3:5, HCSB)

3.   He presents us with partial truth. It was true that they would know good and evil, but Satan deceived them by making them discontent with what they had and created a lust for something forbidden. They did end up gaining some knowledge of sin by experience. They did not become gods. Satan presented them with the same temptation that he fell for - the desire to be as God.

4.   He makes us doubt the goodness of God. He made Adam and Eve feel like God was withholding something good from them.

5.   He makes the forbidden look desirable.

     "I will ascend above the highest clouds; I will make myself like the Most High." (Isa. 14:14, HCSB)

Satan wanted to lead them down the path that he had already taken. He was tempting them to commit the primary sin. Satan wanted to be like God. He did not attain this, and neither did Adam and Eve.

> "Then the woman saw that the tree was good for food and delightful to look at, and that it was desirable for obtaining wisdom. So she took some of its fruit and ate it; she also gave some to her husband, who was with her, and he ate it." (Gen. 3:6, HCSB)

The devil tempted Eve by appealing to her five different senses. She listened to the devil (hearing); she saw the tree was good for food (taste); she saw it was pleasant to the eyes (sight); she took the fruit (touch); and it likely had a lovely scent (smell).

Satan was appealing to the lust of the eyes, the flesh, and the pride of life.

> "[16] For everything that belongs to the world – the lust of the flesh, the lust of the eyes, and the pride in one's lifestyle – is not from the Father, but is from the world. [17]And the world with its lust is passing away, but the one who does God's will remains forever." (1 John 2: 16-17, HCSB)

"[14] But each person is tempted when he is drawn away and enticed by his own evil desires. [15] Then after desire has conceived, it gives birth to sin, and when sin is fully grown, it gives birth to death." (Jam. 1:14-15, HCSB)

LUST – TEMPTATION – ENTICEMENT – SIN – DEATH

Sin is conceived when lust and temptation come together and we give into them. If we provide the right medium, sin will continue to grow in us. When sin matures, it leads to death. The answer to this is only in clinging to the Holy Spirit. Only He can help us weed out our lust. Only He can give us the grace to 'Go and sin no more'.

Do you have an addiction? Confess your sins and the blood of Jesus will cleanse you. Walk in the Spirit, and He will give you the grace to flee from sin.

The Holy Spirit knows us personally and that is why He is able to help us in our weaknesses. Praying in the Spirit (praying in tongues) will cause the Spirit to pray through us. He edifies us (builds us up) so that we can walk in victory.

BLINDED MINDS

THE FALL FROM GLORY

"Both the man and his wife were naked, yet felt no shame." (Gen. 2:25, HCSB)

The word 'ashamed' means 'to be regretful or remorseful'. Shame is not to be associated with shyness and blushing, but is akin to feeling 'paleness and terror'. Psalm 8 describes the state of man before the Fall.

"You made him little less than God and crowned him with glory and honor."
(Ps. 8: 5, HCSB)

Adam and Eve were covered with glory and honor as a garment. So, even though they were naked, they had no cause to be ashamed. They were good, and the glory was their covering.

The knowledge (by experience) of sin caused them to fall from the glory of God. All who were born after them were born in the sinful state. Even David in Psalm 51 acknowledges that he was 'conceived in sin'.

"For all have sinned and fall short of the glory of God." (Rom. 3: 23, HCSB)

MENTAL SHIFT

As soon as they sinned, their spirits died. Before the fall, Adam was a spiritual man. Adam's spirit was submitted to the Lordship of the Holy Spirit. As he walked with God every day, God imparted His wisdom to Adam as the Holy Spirit communed with Adam's spirit . He was spiritually minded. Adam's spirit had dominion over his mind, thereby keeping his flesh in subjection to God's ways. Once his spirit died, he became a natural man, subject to the passions and desires of the flesh. From that time forward he was ruled by the mind of the flesh. Once Adam and Eve were stripped of the glory of God, the eyes of their minds were opened to the miserable state of the knowledge (acquaintance) of evil.

"For the mind-set of the flesh is death, but the mind-set of the Spirit is life and peace."
(Rom. 8:6, HCSB)

We can have one of two mindsets – the Mind of the flesh (which is sense and reason without the Holy Spirit); or the Mind that is influenced by the Holy Spirit.

"Then the eyes of both of them were opened, and they knew they were naked; so they sewed fig leaves together and made loincloths for themselves." (Gen. 3:7, HCSB)

Their physical eyes were already open. What does it mean when it says that their eyes were opened after eating the fruit? The eyes of their minds were opened, and they were now driven by reasoning apart from God. All they saw was their misery, and they were ashamed of their nakedness.

RETURN TO GLORY

Paul the Apostle gave us the whole story when he quoted Psalm 8 when writing Hebrews 2:6-10.

"⁶But one has somewhere testified: What is man that You remember him, or the son of man that You care for him? ⁷ You made him lower than the angels for a short time; You crowned him with glory and honor ⁸ and subjected everything under his feet..." (Heb. 2: 6-8, HCSB)

This is a description of how God made Adam and crowned him with glory and honor. God gave him dominion over the birds of the air and the fish of the sea. Adam lost it when he fell for Satan's temptation. Satan then became the ruler of this world. Jesus, who was born in the likeness of Adam, conquered Satan and regained the lost dominion, glory, and honor.

"⁹ But we do see Jesus – made lower than the angels for a short time so that by God's grace He might taste death for everyone – crowned with glory and honor because of His suffering in death." (Heb. 2: 9, HCSB)

Jesus came in the likeness of sinful flesh, and paid the redemption price with His pure, sinless blood. He has restored us spiritually, and we are seated in heavenly places with Christ. The final stage of redemption will be complete when we gain our glorified bodies at rapture.

"¹⁰ For in bringing many sons to glory, it was entirely appropriate that God – all things exist for Him and through Him – should make the source of their salvation perfect through sufferings." (Heb. 2: 10, HCSB)

Adam lost this crowning glory. Through His death, Jesus restored the fallen human race back to glory. Those who are in Christ can now share in this ever-increasing glory. "In their case, the god of this age has blinded the minds of the unbelievers so they cannot see the light of the gospel of the glory of Christ, who is the image of God." (2 Cor. 4:4, HCSB)

The mind of the natural man is blinded, so he cannot see the glory of Christ. He cannot grasp spiritual revelation. Revelation is transferred from the Holy Spirit to man's spirit. What we receive and believe in our hearts influences the way we think. The thoughts of our mind will influence our actions in the flesh.

"7 Now if the ministry of death, chiseled in letters on stones, came with glory, so that the Israelites were not able to look directly at Moses' face because of the glory from his face – a fading glory…" (2 Cor. 3: 7, HCSB)

"For if the ministry of condemnation had glory, the ministry of righteousness overflows with even more glory." (2 Cor. 3: 9, HCSB)

"…but their minds were closed. For to this day, at the reading of the old covenant, the same veil remains; it is not lifted, because it is set aside only in Christ." (2 Cor. 3: 14, HCSB)

The veil remains upon the unbeliever's heart. His mind is thus blinded, and he cannot see the excellent glory of Christ.

"16…but whenever a person turns to the Lord, the veil is removed. 17 Now the Lord is the Spirit, and where the Spirit of the Lord is, there is freedom." (2 Cor. 3: 16-17, HCSB)

When the person turns to the Holy Spirit and is born again, the veil is removed and his eyes are no longer blinded. He is able to see the glory of God with the eyes of his spirit-governed mind.

"We all, with unveiled faces, are looking as in a mirror at the glory of the Lord and are being transformed into the same image from glory to glory; this is from the Lord who is the Spirit." (2 Cor. 3: 18, HCSB)

As we look into the Word, we behold the beauty and glory of the Lord. The Holy Spirit gives us revelation of Christ in the Old and New Testament. The revelation of Christ changes us into His image. We are transformed (*metamorphoo*) into His image with ever-increasing glory.

MIND TRANSFORMATION

When a person is born again, his mind does not get renewed automatically. The spirit has been regenerated, but the mind needs to be reprogrammed.

"Therefore, brothers, by the mercies of God, I urge you to present your bodies as a living sacrifice, holy and pleasing to God; this is your spiritual worship. 2 Do not be conformed to this age, but be transformed by the renewing of your mind, so that you may discern what is the good, pleasing, and perfect will of God." (Rom. 12: 1-2, HCSB)

RENEWAL

The word 'renewal' implies a 'renovation or a complete change for the better'. Our spirit is in communion with God, but there is a war raging on the battleground of the believer's soul. The flesh and the spirit are pulling at our mind to gain dominion. The outcome of this battle determines whether we are carnally or spiritually minded. The spirit of the Christian is meant to be governed by the Holy Spirit. Under His Lordship, the believer's mind will be renewed daily, as he reads the Word. We are being transformed (*metamorphoo*) into the image of Christ. Our bodies are to be offered as living sacrifices unto God.

> "For those who live according to the flesh think about the things of the flesh, but those who live according to the Spirit, about the things of the Spirit." (Rom. 8: 5, HCSB)

If the things of the Spirit are precious to us, we will dedicate our minds to pursue spiritual things. We will only think, read and watch things that edify and build our spirit. Does this mean that we will never have bad thoughts? While we are in this world, we will always be barraged by evil thoughts. Our responsibility is to not dwell on them. Test the thought against the Word, and eject it if it does not meet the standard. Let the Word be a gatekeeper to our Minds. Let it be the standard by which we can distinguish between the holy and profane.

> "Finally brothers, whatever is true, whatever is honorable, whatever is just, whatever is pure, whatever is lovely, whatever is commendable – if there is any moral excellence and if there is any praise – dwell on these things." (Phil. 4: 8, HCSB)

Do we assess everything that we allow to run through our minds? Is our mind the trash can, or do we treat it as the storehouse for Philippians 4: 8 type of thoughts? Our thinking is affected by whatever we allow our minds to dwell on and this affects who we are.

MIND OF CHRIST

We have all heard that we must have the mind of Christ, but what does that mean to us?

How can we receive the mind of Christ? It may seem too difficult for us to attain, possibly even unimaginable. My pastor reminds us that our minds need to be renewed as often as our hair needs to be combed. The mind tends to default to its original fleshly thought patterns. This is why it must be renewed daily.

MIND OF THE FLESH VERSUS MIND OF THE SPIRIT

> "⁶For the mind-set of the flesh is death, but the mind-set of the Spirit is life and peace. ⁷For the mind-set of the flesh is hostile to God because it does not submit itself to God's law, for it is unable to do so." (Rom. 8: 6 -7, HCSB)

The verse above shows us that the result of Spirit-filled thinking is life and peace. Do you want life and peace? Read the word and ask the Spirit to align your thoughts to Christ's. We have either one of two mindsets. It depends on what we are feeding our minds. We must daily choose whether to have the mind of the flesh or the mind of Christ.

HIDDEN WISDOM REVEALED

> "⁷On the contrary, we speak God's hidden wisdom in a mystery, a wisdom God predestined before the ages for our glory. ⁸None of the rulers of this age knew this wisdom, for if they had known it, they would not have crucified the Lord of glory." (1 Cor. 2:7-8, HCSB)

This mystery of Christ was hidden through the ages, and was only revealed to the apostles by the Holy Spirit. Only the spiritual man receives such enlightenment. This wisdom is foolishness to the unregenerate man. If we seek after His words as we would for hidden treasure the Spirit of revelation will illuminate our minds.

> "But as it is written: What eye did not see and ear did not hear, and what never entered the human mind – God prepared this for those who love Him." (1 Cor. 2: 9, HCSB)

> "¹⁰Now God has revealed these things to us by the Spirit, for the Spirit searches everything, even the depths of God. ¹¹ For who among men knows the thoughts of a man except the spirit of the man that is in him? In the same way, no one knows the thoughts of God except the Spirit of God. ¹² Now we have not received the spirit of the world, but the Spirit who comes from God, so that we may understand what has been freely given to us by God. ¹³ We also speak these things, not in words

taught by human wisdom, but in those taught by the Spirit, explaining spiritual things to spiritual people. [14] But the unbeliever does not welcome what comes from God's Spirit, because it is foolishness to him; he is not able to understand it since it is evaluated spiritually. [15] The spiritual person, however, can evaluate everything, yet he himself cannot be evaluated by anyone. [16] For who has known the Lord's mind, that he may instruct Him? But we have the mind of Christ." (1 Cor. 2: 10-16, HCSB)

The apostle adds that we have the mind of Christ, and the mind of Christ is the mind of God. Jesus is God, the principal messenger and prophet of God. The apostles were empowered by His Spirit to make known His mind to us. In the Holy Scriptures, the mind of Christ and the mind of God are fully revealed to us. Observe, it is the great privilege of Christians that they have the mind of Christ revealed to them by His Spirit.

The mind of the Flesh:
- Is death
- Is blinded
- Cannot see the glory of Christ

The mind of the Holy Spirit:
- Is life and peace
- Has unveiled eyes
- Beholds the glory of Christ
- Is being transformed into His image by the Spirit

Two Minds

THE LAW OF SIN AND DEATH

"Therefore, no condemnation now exists for those in Christ Jesus..." (Rom.8:1, HCSB)

To be free from condemnation before God, there are two requirements – we must be in Christ and we must walk after the Holy Spirit.

THE LAW OF THE SPIRIT OF LIFE

"...because the Spirit's law of life in Christ Jesus has set you free from the law of sin and of death." (Rom.8:2, HCSB)

THE LAW OF SIN AND DEATH

This is the Law of Moses – derived from the Ten Commandments. Does this Law bring salvation? No! The Law can never be fully obeyed by the sinful man. When man tries to obey it, he is found to be a lawbreaker.

"For whoever keeps the entire law, yet fails in one point, is guilty of breaking it all" (Jam. 2:10, HCSB)

"[10] For all who rely on the works of the law are under a curse, because it is written: Everyone who does not continue doing everything written in the book of the law is cursed. [11] Now it is clear that no one is justified before God by the law, because the righteous will live by faith." (Gal. 3:10-11, HCSB)

What is the purpose of the Law? Galatians 3:21-29 sheds a light on the purpose of the Law as being a way to bring us to Christ and it shows us that we are slaves to sin. We can only be justified by faith in Christ, not by our own righteous works.

MARRIAGE PARALLEL

Paul compares the relationship between sinful man and the Law to marriage.

"For when we were in the flesh, the sinful passions operated through the law in every part of us and bore fruit for death." (Rom. 7: 5, HCSB)

Man + Law = Death

Is the Law sinful? No. It is holy. When man and the Law unite the fruit is death, because it awakens man's desire to sin. Sin gives birth to death.

> "What should we say then? Is the law sin? Absolutely not! On the contrary, I would not have known sin if it were not for the law. For example, I would not have known what it is to covet if the law had not said, "Do not covet." (Rom. 7: 7, HCSB)

Who is at fault? The fault lies in sin working within us. The Law brings to light the 'sin' principle working in us. This sin was bequeathed by Adam to the human race. Adam's sons were made in his likeness. They all had dead spirits and were shaped in iniquity and conceived in sin.

> "Indeed, I was guilty when I was born; I was sinful when my mother conceived me." (Ps. 51: 5, HCSB)

> "And sin, seizing an opportunity through the commandment, produced in me coveting of every kind. For apart from the law sin is dead." (Rom. 7: 8, HCSB)

SIN PUTS US TO DEATH

Man's sins are brought to the surface when the Law highlights them. This is why we innately want to do things that are forbidden. The prohibitive Law evokes a desire in us to sin, that we would not have otherwise had.

> "⁹Once I was alive apart from the law, but when the commandment came, sin sprang to life ¹⁰ and I died. The commandment that was meant for life resulted in death for me." (Rom. 7: 9-10, HCSB)

Jesus terminated the marriage between us and the Law in Romans 7:1-4. If a married woman marries another man, she is an adulteress. If her husband is dead, the marriage law does not bind her. If she then marries another man, she will not be an adulteress. In the same way, we have become dead to the Law. We who are born of the Spirit are married to Christ.

LAW OF THE SPIRIT OF LIFE

> "⁴Therefore, my brothers, you also were put to death in relation to the law through the crucified body of the Messiah, so that you may belong to another – to Him who was raised from the dead – that we may bear fruit for God. ⁵ For when we were in the flesh, the sinful passions operated through the law in every part of us and bore fruit for death. ⁶ But now we have been released from the law, since we have died to what held us, so that we may serve in the new way of the Spirit and not in the old letter of the law." (Rom. 7: 4-6, HCSB)

When we obey the promptings of the Holy Spirit we are obeying and fulfilling the Law of the Spirit. For instance, The Law of Sin and Death states "Thou shalt not commit adultery" and the Law of the Spirit states "He who lusts after a woman in his heart has committed adultery." (Exodus 20:14 and Matthew 5:27-28, HCSB)

This example shows us that the Law of the Spirit has a higher standard than the Law of Sin and Death. Under the Law, if you were caught in the act of adultery, you were stoned. While under the Law of the Spirit, lust in one's heart is considered adultery. If we follow the leading of the Holy Spirit, He will deal with the root of our problems. He judges the thoughts of our hearts.

In another example, The Law of Sin and Death instructs us to 'pay tithes' and the Law of the Spirit directs us to 'give generously', as in 1 Tim 6:17-18. The Law of the Spirit actually goes over and above the Law. Observing the Law is just about going through the motions, but the Law of the Spirit deals with the very heart of the matter. When we obey the Law of the Spirit, our hearts will always be right before God, and we will do what is right.

THE LAW CANNOT REDEEM

"What the law could not do since it was limited by the flesh, God did. He condemned sin in the flesh by sending His own Son in flesh like ours under sin's domain, and as a sin offering…" (Rom. 8:3, HCSB)

"Keep My statutes and ordinances; a person will live if he does them. I am *Yahweh*." (Lev. 18:5, HCSB)

The Law was designed to bring life to those who obeyed it completely. No man could fulfill the Law because of Sin reigning in him. The man who breaks even a single commandment is guilty of breaking the whole Law. Therefore, the Law could not redeem man. Jesus came and fulfilled the Law. Hence, we do not disregard the Law altogether. When we obey the law of the Spirit, we will fulfill the Law.

"Don't assume that I came to destroy the Law or the Prophets. I did not come to destroy but to fulfill." (Matt. 5:17, HCSB)

Let us travel back to a parallel in the book of Ruth from the Old Testament.

RUTH AND BOAZ

To understand the story better, let us study the concept of levirate marriage and the law of the 'kinsman redeemer'. The word 'redeem' implies to purchase back; to liberate; or rescue from captivity or bondage. If an Israelite man died without an heir, his brother was supposed to marry the widow and raise their children in the name of the deceased. This concept of a levirate marriage was practiced to prevent the extinction of a branch of a family. The Hebrew word for kinsman is *ga'al* (and means "to redeem, to be the next of kin (and as such to buy back a relative's property, marry his widow, etc.): avenge, deliver, purchase, ransom, revenger.")

If a family was in financial trouble, a richer family member could step forward and buy the land for them. This man was known as the kinsman redeemer. This land would return to the original owner in the year of Jubilee.

Naomi was desolate and in financial trouble. She had lost her husband and sons. She was left with Ruth. Naomi said that Boaz was the kinsman, but Boaz knew that there was a closer kinsman. The onus of redemption would fall on this man. If this man refused the right to redeem the land, Boaz would be the next in line.

"[12] Yes, it is true that I am a family redeemer, but there is a redeemer closer than I am. [13] Stay here tonight, and in the morning, if he wants to redeem you, that's good.

Let him redeem you. But if he doesn't want to redeem you, as the Lord lives, I will. Now lie down until morning." (Ruth 3:12-13, HCSB)

Boaz approached the man the next morning in front of the elders of the city.

"³He said to the redeemer, Naomi, who has returned from the land of Moab, is selling a piece of land that belonged to our brother Elimelech. ⁴ I thought I should inform you: Buy it back in the presence of those seated here and in the presence of the elders of my people. If you want to redeem it, do so. But if you do not want to redeem it, tell me so that I will know, because there isn't anyone other than you to redeem it, and I am next after you." "I want to redeem it," he answered. ⁵Then Boaz said, "On the day you buy the land from Naomi, you will also acquire Ruth the Moabitess, the wife of the deceased man, to perpetuate the man's name on his property." ⁶The redeemer replied, "I can't redeem it myself, or I will ruin my own inheritance. Take my right of redemption, because I can't redeem it."" (Ruth 4:3-6, HCSB)

The kinsman may not have wanted to spend money to buy a plot of land that would eventually pass down to the heir who would be born in Elimelech's line. This is possibly why he was afraid of diluting his inheritance.

In Ruth 4:9-10, Boaz agreed to redeem the land and purchase Ruth the Moabite to be his wife. This is but a shadow of the story of redemption. Similarly, Jesus is our kinsman redeemer. We are the gentile bride that He has purchased with His own blood. The nearer kinsman who could not redeem the land is a type of the Law. The Holy Law is unable to redeem us from the slavery of sin. Consequently, it is rendered 'weak' by the flesh (the entire nature of man without the Holy Spirit). Once we are redeemed and led by the Holy Spirit, we fulfill the demands of the Law when we obey His prompting.

"...in order that the law's requirement would be accomplished in us who do not walk according to the flesh but according to the Spirit." (Rom. 8:4, HCSB)

We have two options. We can either obey the dictates of the flesh or we can obey the commands of the Spirit. If we walk in the flesh, we cannot fulfill the Law; but if we walk in the Spirit, we will fulfill the righteous requirement of the Law.

WORKS VERSUS FAITH

"Are you so foolish? After beginning with the Spirit, are you now going to be made complete by the flesh?" (Gal. 3:3, HCSB)

Paul wrote this letter to the Galatians because the Jewish believers were compelling the Gentile believers to be circumcised. They were mixing the Gospel with the Law. They were trying to bind them to the Law. Having begun new life in the Spirit, believers tend to fall back into legalism, focusing on doing the works of the Law rather than living by faith. In doing so, they disregard the grace that saves. Our liberty in the Spirit is threatened by legalism. Paul presents an argument stating that having started in the Spirit, we must continue to walk by faith in the Spirit. Since the Galatians went off course, Paul redirected them by going back to the beginning.

JUSTICATION

"...know that no one is justified by the works of the law but by faith in Jesus Christ. And we have believed in Christ Jesus so that we might be justified by faith in Christ and not by the works of the law, because by the works of the law no human being will be justified." (Gal. 2:16, HCSB)

Jesus paid the price for our justification. There is nothing that we can add to His work. The Galatians were trying to 'complete' their salvation, by adding circumcision to their to-do list. Jesus' work is perfect and complete. We just have to believe and have faith in the work of Christ. It may seem too simple, but it is all that God requires of us. To try and justify ourselves through works is to imply that Jesus' sacrifice is insufficient and incomplete. It is with good reason that Christ proclaimed, in John 19:30 (HCSB), "It is finished."

RECEIVING THE SPIRIT

"I went up according to a revelation and presented to them the gospel I preach among the Gentiles – but privately to those recognized as leaders – so that I might not be running, or have run the race, in vain." (Gal. 2:2, HCSB)

Since the Galatians were being swayed by winds of doctrine, Paul redirected them to their original salvation experience. The Jews believed that they were the physical seed of Abraham. Since circumcision was a sign of the Abrahamic covenant, they felt like they were straying from the covenant handed down from the fathers. Paul showed them that the spiritual sons of Abraham inherited the promises associated with the Abrahamic covenant by faith alone. Abraham received righteousness by faith, before he was circumcised.

RIGHTEOUSNESS BY BELIEF ONLY

> "Just as Abraham believed God, and it was credited to him for righteousness..." (Gal. 3:6, HCSB)

> "¹⁰For all who rely on the works of the law are under a curse, because it is written: Everyone who does not continue doing everything written in the book of the law is cursed. ¹¹Now it is clear that no one is justified before God by the law, because the righteous will live by faith.¹² But the law is not based on faith; instead, the one who does these things will live by them." (Gal. 3:10-12, HCSB)

Verse 10 states that all that rely on the works of the law are under a curse, because everyone is a lawbreaker. All lawbreakers fall short of the glory of God. The Law has nothing to do with faith. We cannot mix the two. When we live by faith, and obey the prompting of the Spirit, He will enable us to fulfill the Law of the Spirit, which is above and beyond the Law of Sin and Death.

REDEMPTION

> "¹³ Christ has redeemed us from the curse of the law by becoming a curse for us, because it is written: Everyone who is hung on a tree is cursed.¹⁴ The purpose was that the blessing of Abraham would come to the Gentiles by Christ Jesus, so that we could receive the promised Spirit through faith." (Gal. 3:13-14, HCSB)

THE PROMISE

Abraham believed God and it was accounted to him as righteousness. He received the promise that the Gentiles would be blessed through him.

> "Now the Scripture saw in advance that God would justify the Gentiles by faith and told the good news ahead of time to Abraham, saying, All the nations will be blessed through you." (Gal. 3:8, HCSB)

> "¹⁶ Now the promises were spoken to Abraham and to his seed. He does not say "and to seeds," as though referring to many, but referring to one, and to your seed, who is Christ. ¹⁷ And I say this: The law, which came 430 years later, does not revoke a covenant that was previously ratified by God and cancel the promise. ¹⁸ For if the inheritance is from the law, it is no longer from the promise; but God granted it to Abraham through the promise." (Gal. 3:16-18, HCSB)

Verses 16 and 17 tell us that the promise came before the law. The Law does not make void the promise. Verse 18 conveys that the inheritance of the promise does not depend on observing the Law.

"...then understand that those who have faith are Abraham's sons..." (Gal. 3: 7, HCSB)

"¹³ For the promise to Abraham or to his descendants that he would inherit the world was not through the law, but through the righteousness that comes by faith. ¹⁴ If those who are of the law are heirs, faith is made empty and the promise is canceled." (Rom. 4: 13-14, HCSB)

The promise has nothing to do with the Law. So what was the purpose of the Law? Galatians 3:19 explains that the purpose is to disclose guilt; to make man conscious of sin; to be in effect till the Seed should come and verse 24 describes how the Law is our trainer and guardian.

HEIRS OF THE PROMISE

"²³Before this faith came, we were confined under the law, imprisoned until the coming faith was revealed. ²⁴The law, then, was our guardian until Christ, so that we could be justified by faith. ²⁵But since that faith has come, we are no longer under a guardian, ²⁶for you are all sons of God through faith in Christ Jesus. ²⁷For as many of you as have been baptized into Christ have put on Christ like a garment. ²⁸There is no Jew or Greek, slave or free, male or female; for you are all one in Christ Jesus. And if you belong to Christ, then you are Abraham's seed, heirs according to the promise." (Gal. 3: 23-29, HCSB)

"Now I say that as long as the heir is a child, he differs in no way from a slave, though he is the owner of everything. ² Instead, he is under guardians and stewards until the time set by his father." (Gal. 4:1-2, HCSB)

What time is this passage speaking of?

"⁴ When the time came to completion, God sent His Son, born of a woman, born under the law, ⁵ to redeem those under the law, so that we might receive adoption as sons. ⁶ And because you are sons, God has sent the Spirit of His Son into our hearts, crying, *Abba*, Father!" (Gal. 4: 4-6, HCSB)

Paul is showing the Galatians, that they received the Spirit of son-ship because of their faith, and not because they fulfilled the works of the Law. We are saved by faith. We receive the Spirit, and are heirs of the promise by faith alone. The Law was our tutor till the time of Christ. Now, Grace is our tutor.

FROM LEGALISM TO LIBERTY

"You who are trying to be justified by the law are alienated from Christ; you have fallen from grace." (Gal. 5:4, HCSB)

FROM LAW TO GRACE

"Now the Lord is the Spirit, and where the Spirit of the Lord is, there is freedom." (2 Cor. 3:17, HCSB)

The Law or Old Covenant is called the "Ministration of Death." Under the New Covenant, we do not have to legalistically fulfill the Law. We heed the voice or the promptings of the Holy Spirit and so obey the Law of the Spirit of Life.

The Law Vs. The Promise to Abraham

The Law	Promise
Given to Moses	Given to Abraham
Demands righteousness	Righteousness is imparted
Works based	Faith based
No salvation	Salvation through the Seed of Abraham
Cannot make void the promise	Promise came before the Law
All who depend on the Law are cursed	Sons of faith inherit the blessing of the Spirit
Legalism	Liberty

TWO MOUNTAINS

Mount Zion and Mount Sinai represent the Old and New Covenants. We have moved from one to the other by grace.

"²¹ Tell me, those of you who want to be under the law, don't you hear the law? ²² For it is written that Abraham had two sons, one by a slave and the other by a free woman. ²³But the one by the slave was born according to the impulse of the flesh, while the one by the free woman was born as the result of a promise. ²⁴These things are illustrations, for the women represent the two covenants. One is from Mount Sinai and bears children into slavery – this is Hagar. ²⁵ Now Hagar is Mount Sinai in Arabia and corresponds to the present Jerusalem, for she is in slavery with her children. ²⁶ But the Jerusalem above is free, and she is our mother." (Gal. 4:21-26, HCSB)

The analogy is simple: Mount Sinai is likened to Hagar the slave, while Mount Zion is compared to Sarah the free woman. Those who are under the Law of Sin and Death are in bondage to it, while those who follow the Law of the Spirit of life are free because the Holy Spirit will always lead us into liberty.

> [28] Now you, brothers, like Isaac, are children of promise. [29] But just as then the child born according to the flesh persecuted the one born according to the Spirit, so also now. [30] But what does the Scripture say? Drive out the slave and her son, for the son of the slave will never be a coheir with the son of the free woman. [31]Therefore, brothers, we are not children of the slave but of the free woman." (Gal. 4:28-31, HCSB)

The Galatians were set free from the bondage of the Law by the Holy Spirit. They later yoked themselves to the Law again, trying to mix both Law and Grace. We will fall from grace if we seek to be justified by the Law. Choose to be an Isaac not Ishmael, for the inheritance of the son of promise is more excellent. Jesus has set us free from the bondage of the Law, so enjoy the freedom of righteous living as you follow the Holy Spirit.

ZION IS HEAVENLY JERUSALEM

> "For you have not come to what could be touched, to a blazing fire, to darkness, gloom, and storm..." (Heb. 12:18, HCSB)

> "[22] Instead, you have come to Mount Zion, to the city of the living God (the heavenly Jerusalem), to myriads of angels in festive gathering, [23] to the assembly of the firstborn whose names have been written in heaven, to God who is the Judge of all, to the spirits of righteous people made perfect, [24] to Jesus (mediator of a new covenant), and to the sprinkled blood, which says better things than the blood of Abel." (Heb. 12:22-24, HCSB)

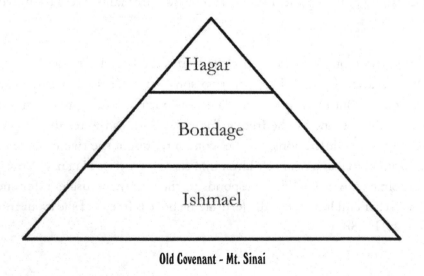

Old Covenant - Mt. Sinai

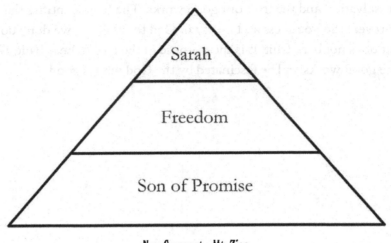

New Covenant - Mt. Zion

GRACE

The Holy Spirit is called the Spirit of Grace. The word 'Grace' (*Charis*) represents 'good will, loving-kindness, and good favor'. Grace is the merciful kindness by which God, exerting his holy influence upon souls, turns them to Christ. He keeps, strengthens, and increases them in Christian faith, knowledge, and affection, and kindles them to the exercise of the Christian virtues.

GRACE AND WORKS

Does salvation depend on works? Are we supposed to do good works? If our salvation does not depend on it, then why are they necessary?

> "...made us alive with the Messiah even though we were dead in trespasses. You are saved by grace!" (Eph. 2:5, HCSB)

> "⁸ For you are saved by grace through faith, and this is not from yourselves; it is God's gift – ⁹ not from works, so that no one can boast." (Eph. 2:8-9, HCSB)

It is clear from these verses that only grace through faith saves us. Salvation is a free gift. Our works cannot save us. Even when we were unlovable Christ died for us. He loved us first. Even the faith to be saved is given by Him. We have nothing to boast about now. It is all because of Him. Our righteousness is as filthy rags - our 'good' works cannot purchase salvation. How do good works fit into the picture?

> "For we are His creation, created in Christ Jesus for good works, which God prepared ahead of time so that we should walk in them." (Eph. 2:10, HCSB)

Christ has saved us. Once we are saved, we are meant to do good works that shine the light of Christ. A Christian who does good works can be equated to a tree bearing fruit. The roots of the tree represent our salvation and the fruit our good works. The fruit identifies the tree. In the same way, good works reveal the goodness and mercy of God to others. If we don't do good works, we are like a tree that does not bear fruit. It is the purpose of the tree to bear fruit. Bear good fruit so people will see the good works and be fascinated by the God who is good.

"The Word became flesh and took up residence among us. We observed His glory, the glory as the One and Only Son from the Father, full of grace and truth." (John 1:14, HCSB)

"Indeed, we have all received grace after grace from His fullness..." (John 1:16, HCSB)

Grace is revealed to us in the person of Jesus Christ. He showed mercy to a world that only knew judgement. Before then, grace was not known at all.

"...for the law was given through Moses, grace and truth came through Jesus Christ." (John 1:17)

Jesus took us out of the Age of the Law into the Age of Grace.

THE WOMAN CAUGHT IN ADULTERY

"[5] In the law Moses commanded us to stone such women. So what do You say?" [6] They asked this to trap Him, in order that they might have evidence to accuse Him. Jesus stooped down and started writing on the ground with His finger. [7] When they persisted in questioning Him, He stood up and said to them, "The one without sin among you should be the first to throw a stone at her." [8] Then He stooped down again and continued writing on the ground. [9] When they heard this, they left one by one, starting with the older men. Only He was left, with the woman in the center. [10] When Jesus stood up, He said to her, "Woman, where are they? Has no one condemned you?" [11] "No one, Lord," she answered. "Neither do I condemn you," said Jesus. "Go, and from now on do not sin anymore."" (John 8:5-11, HCSB)

The Pharisees were attempting to trap Jesus. They were hoping He would break the Law. They thought they were judging the adulteress according to the Law, but their judgement was unjust.

"If a man is discovered having sexual relations with another man's wife, both the man who had sex with the woman and the woman must die. You must purge the evil from Israel." (Deut. 22:22, HCSB)

The Pharisees did not judge her correctly. She was indeed an adulteress and deserved to be stoned. They neglected to bring the man who was with her. Proverbs 11:1 states that unjust scales are an abomination to the Lord. Jesus appeared to be breaking the Law by letting her go free. Actually, He was showing everyone that they were all in the same standing as her. That was the very purpose of the Law. They were all lawbreakers. None were sinless and the Law proved just that. James gives us insight into this matter.

"⁸ Indeed, if you keep the royal law prescribed in the Scripture, Love your neighbor as yourself, you are doing well. ⁹ But if you show favoritism, you commit sin and are convicted by the law as transgressors. ¹⁰ For whoever keeps the entire law, yet fails in one point, is guilty of breaking it all. ¹¹ For He who said, Do not commit adultery, also said, Do not murder. So if you do not commit adultery, but you do murder, you are a lawbreaker. ¹² Speak and act as those who will be judged by the law of freedom. ¹³ For judgment is without mercy to the one who hasn't shown mercy. Mercy triumphs over judgment." (Jam. 2:8-13, HCSB)

"There is no mercy in the Law. Mercy through grace will triumph over the Law because the demands of the law have been met by grace. Lawbreakers are justified by grace through faith to escape the judgement of the Law." (Dake's Bible)[1]

STONY HEART FOR HEART OF FLESH

"²⁵ I will also sprinkle clean water on you, and you will be clean. I will cleanse you from all your impurities and all your idols. ²⁶ I will give you a new heart and put a new spirit within you; I will remove your heart of stone and give you a heart of flesh. ²⁷ I will place My Spirit within you and cause you to follow My statutes and carefully observe My ordinances. ²⁸ Then you will live in the land that I gave your fathers; you will be My people, and I will be your God." (Ezek. 36:25-28, HCSB)

God had previously written with His finger on stone tablets, representing the stony hearts of man.

"When He finished speaking with Moses on Mount Sinai, He gave him the two tablets of the testimony, stone tablets inscribed by the finger of God." (Ex. 31:18, HCSB)

When Jesus wrote with His finger in the mud, He was ushering in the New Covenant, the words of which are written on fleshly hearts.

NEW COVENANT

"³¹ "Look, the days are coming" – this is the Lord's declaration – "when I will make a new covenant with the house of Israel and with the house of Judah. ³² This one will not be like the covenant I made with their ancestors when I took them by the hand to bring them out of the land of Egypt – a covenant they broke even though I had married them" – the LORD's declaration. ³³ "Instead, this is the covenant I will make with the house of Israel after those days" – the Lord's declaration. "I will put My teaching within them and write it on their hearts. I will be their God, and they

124 • Life, Liberty and the Pursuit of the Holy Spirit

will be My people. ³⁴ No longer will one teach his neighbor or his brother, saying, 'Know the Lord,' for they will all know Me, from the least to the greatest of them" – this is the Lord's declaration. "For I will forgive their wrongdoing and never again remember their sin.'" (Jer. 31:31-34, HCSB)

Under the New Covenant, God sends the Holy Spirit into the heart of the believer. The Holy Spirit will inscribe His Law in our hearts. As we obey His promptings, we will obey the Law of the Spirit of Life in Christ Jesus.

GRACE – THE CURE FOR CARNALITY

Have you ever wondered how to cure your rebellious flesh? Have you tried to suppress it and bring it under your control? It seems like nothing can tame our fleshly desires. Just when you think the fleshly appetite is under control, the slightest trigger causes it to rear its ugly head.

It is comforting to know that even the apostle Paul was caught in this battle. The soul is a battleground. We constantly have to make a choice – either to obey the dictates of the flesh or the promptings of the Spirit. Our battle with the flesh is ongoing. How can we not give into the dictates of the flesh? Who shall deliver us from the body of sin? As Paul quotes in Romans 7:24-25, Jesus Christ our Lord. It is His Grace that will teach us to walk in the Spirit and deny the lusts of the flesh.

> "¹¹For the grace of God has appeared with salvation for all people, ¹²instructing us to deny godlessness and worldly lusts and to live in a sensible, righteous, and godly way in the present age…" (Titus 2:11-12, HCSB)

> "The law, then, was our guardian until Christ, so that we could be justified by faith." (Gal. 3:24, HCSB)

Previously the Law was our trainer, showing us the difference between right and wrong. It did not give us a cure for sin in us. Now that we are not slaves to sin (but to righteousness), Grace gives us the ability to renounce ungodliness. Grace is our new tutor, teaching us to live a godly life. Jesus told the woman to, "Go and sin no more" (John 8:11, HCSB). His words spoken to her heart gave her the ability to overcome her adulterous lifestyle. In the same way, when we get into the presence of Jesus, His Spirit speaks the words of Grace to our hearts, which will empower us to live self-controlled and godly lives today!

Grace! Grace! God's Grace! How much we need His Grace!

ESTHER AND HEGAI

"⁸ When the king's command and edict became public knowledge, many young women gathered at the fortress of Susa under Hegai's care. Esther was also taken to the palace and placed under the care of Hegai, who was in charge of the women. ⁹ The young woman pleased him and gained his favor so that he accelerated the process of the beauty treatments and the special diet that she received. He assigned seven hand-picked female servants to her from the palace and transferred her and her servants to the harem's best quarters." (Esth. 2:8-9, HCSB)

Esther was pleasing (*Yatab*) to Hegai. We learned that Enoch pleased God as he walked with God from Hebrews 11:5. Solomon's speech also pleased the Lord in 1 Kings 3:10.

SEVEN PILLARS OF WISDOM

Esther is a type of the church, the chaste virgin who is espoused to Christ. Just as Esther was placed under the care of Hegai, we are under the counsel of the Holy Spirit. He is our teacher and guide. Jesus will fill us with the sevenfold Spirit of Wisdom if we just turn to Him and ask for wisdom.

> "The Spirit of the Lord will rest on Him – a Spirit of wisdom and understanding, a Spirit of counsel and strength, a Spirit of knowledge and of the fear of the Lord." (Isa. 11:2, HCSB)

When we are filled with the Holy Spirit, we will have the attributes of submitting to the Lordship of God - wisdom, understanding, counsel, might, knowledge, and the fear of the Lord. These are the attributes of the Holy Spirit which were seen in Christ as He was full of the Holy Ghost. The Spirit will impart these qualities to us if we will make room for Him.

> "During the year before each young woman's turn to go to King Ahasuerus, the harem regulation required her to receive beauty treatments with oil of myrrh for six months and then with perfumes and cosmetics for another six months." (Esth. 2:12, HCSB)

The bitter herbs of myrrh represent the times of trouble. God enables us to emerge from life's troubles with the fragrance of Christ. The sweet odors represent the sweet times that only God's blessing bestows on us. These are different articles used to prepare the bride, to refine her faith. This is typical of a believer's life, a lifetime peppered with trials and joys.

> "When the young woman would go to the king, she was given whatever she requested to take with her from the harem to the palace." (Esth. 2:13, HCSB)

God will grant us the desires of our heart. All the riches of our heavenly Father are available to us. However, our lives should not be driven by the pursuit of our desires. The very purpose of our lives should be to seek His face and do His will. Surely we can go deeper than just asking for desires to be fulfilled. Solomon could have asked for riches and glory. Solomon asked for wisdom to rule the people. His prayer pleased the Lord.

> "Esther was the daughter of Abihail, the uncle of Mordecai who had adopted her as his own daughter. When her turn came to go to the king, she did not ask for anything except what Hegai, the king's trusted official in charge of the harem, suggested. Esther won approval in the sight of everyone who saw her." (Esth. 2:15, HCSB)

Esther saw that Hegai knew what was best for her, given his years of experience and wisdom in this area. Hegai knew the tastes of the king, but offered his counsel only when it was asked of him. None of the other women stopped to ask Hegai's opinion. Only Esther wholly submitted herself to his directives regarding her needs. We can be submitted and obedient as Esther was. Most of us are bullheaded and strong-willed and know exactly what we want in life. Esther was different. Her humble attitude paved the pathway for her success, and it befits us to take a leaf out of her book.

> "The king loved Esther more than all the other women. She won more favor and approval from him than did any of the other young women. He placed the royal crown on her head and made her queen in place of Vashti." (Esth. 2:17, HCSB)

Esther obtained grace (*Chen*) and favor (*Cheched*). *Chen* and *cheched* represent goodness, kindness, faithfulness, and in a good sense, zeal toward anyone. Our desire should be to please the Lord. Grace and favor have come to us in Christ. May favor abound to us as we submit to His leading and acknowledge His Lordship.

SECTION 8
GIFTS OF THE SPIRIT

GIFTS BY GRACE

"Now concerning what comes from the Spirit: brothers, I do not want you to be unaware." (1 Cor. 12:1, HCSB)

The gifts (*charisms*) of the Holy Spirit are the special endowments of supernatural energy. The gifts are due to the power of divine grace operating in the soul (of the believer) by the Holy Spirit.

"Now there are different gifts, but the same Spirit." (1 Cor. 12:4, HCSB)

The gifts or extraordinary talents endowed on Christians may vary, but the Holy Spirit stays the same. The *charismata* are a direct result of *charis* (divine grace). We do not possess the gift because of our own merit. They are called the gifts of the Spirit and will only operate when we flow in the Holy Ghost. The abilities were never provided to personally exalt the believer, but to enable more effective service.

HOW ARE THE GIFTS DISTRIBUTED?

"But one and the same Spirit is active in all these, distributing to each person as He wills." (1 Cor. 12:11, HCSB)

Timothy received the gifts from the Holy Spirit when the elders laid hands on him and prophesied at his ordination.

"Do not neglect the gift that is in you; it was given to you through prophecy, with the laying on of hands by the council of elders." (1 Tim. 4:14, HCSB)

Scripture tells us to earnestly desire after gifts so we continually receive the gifts as we grow spiritually.

PURPOSE OF THE GIFTS

"A demonstration of the Spirit is given to each person to produce what is beneficial…" (1 Cor. 12:7, HCSB)

In Greek, the word 'manifestation' means to make visible. The purpose of the gift is to make God known to people and to help and edify people.

DIFFERENT GIFTS, SAME SPIRIT

> "⁵ There are different ministries, but the same Lord. ⁶ And there are different activities, but the same God activates each gift in each person." (1 Cor. 12:5-6, HCSB)

The Holy Spirit is one, but He chooses to work in various ways. Have you ever wondered, "Are the gifts for me?" or "Maybe I'm not good enough for these gifts?" God desires to give every believer the gifts – maybe not all of them, but as much as He wills. We are just vessels that God can use to touch other people. He deems us worthy because He paid for us with His blood. Who can the Spirit use in the operation of the gifts?

> "A demonstration of the Spirit is given to each person to produce what is beneficial…"
> (1 Cor. 12:7, HCSB)

> "Pursue love and desire spiritual gifts, and above all that you may prophesy."
> (1 Cor. 14:1, HCSB)

The two go hand in hand. We must pursue love, otherwise we will be like a clanging cymbal, as described in 1 Cor. 13:1. Ideally, the Christian must be walking in love and operating in the gifts, all the while being led by the Spirit.

> "But desire the greater gifts. And I will show you an even better way." (1 Cor. 12:31, HCSB)

> "So also you – since you are zealous for spiritual gifts, seek to excel in building up the church." (1 Cor. 14:12, HCSB)

REKINDLE THE GIFT OF GOD

We are warned to not be ignorant about the gifts. We must not neglect them, but stir them up so that we will be the most effective servants.

> "Do not neglect the gift that is in you; it was given to you through prophecy, with the laying on of hands by the council of elders." (1 Tim. 4:14, HCSB)

This scripture indicates that spiritual gifts can be neglected. We are told to stir up the gifts to such a great degree as to fan them into flame.

> "Therefore, I remind you to keep ablaze the gift of God that is in you through the laying on of my hands." (2 Tim. 1:6, HCSB)

Rekindling the gift of God can be likened to stirring the dregs found at the bottom of a vessel. When we stir the liquid, the dregs rise to the surface. If the liquid is not stirred, the particles settle to the bottom. They are present in the vessel but not apparently visible. Gifts can 'lie low' for a while if we do not rekindle them.

> "The man who boasts about a gift that does not exist is like clouds and wind without rain." (Pro. 25:14, HCSB)

The gift is never for self-glorification. We need not announce our gifts. God will shine the light on us when He wants us to use the gift. When the gifts of the Spirit are being used by a humble believer, they give the most glory to God. We could all use a dose of humility, don't you think? It is humbling to know that without Him, we are nothing, can do nothing and have nothing. People tend to be put off by pride, even if the gift is truly given by the Spirit. We do not lose control of ourselves when we are operating in the gifts. God is a God of order. The believer is in control of his spirit, as he yields to the Holy Ghost.

> "[32] And the prophets' spirits are under the control of the prophets, [33] since God is not a God of disorder but of peace..." (1 Cor. 14:32-33, HCSB)

The gifts are for the edification of people. They should not cause chaos in the church service.

HOW DO WE USE THE GIFTS?

> "[3] For by the grace given to me, I tell everyone among you not to think of himself more highly than he should think. Instead, think sensibly, as God has distributed a measure of faith to each one. [4] Now as we have many parts in one body, and all the parts do not have the same function, [5] in the same way we who are many are one body in Christ and individually members of one another. [6] According to the grace given to us, we have different gifts: If prophecy, use it according to the standard of one's faith; [7] if service, in service; if teaching, in teaching; [8] if exhorting, in exhortation; giving, with generosity; leading, with diligence; showing mercy, with cheerfulness." (Rom. 12:3-8, HCSB)

"⁴Now there are different gifts, but the same Spirit. ⁵There are different ministries, but the same Lord. ⁶And there are different activities, but the same God activates each gift in each person. ⁷A demonstration of the Spirit is given to each person to produce what is beneficial: ⁸to one is given a message of wisdom through the Spirit, to another, a message of knowledge by the same Spirit, ⁹to another, faith by the same Spirit, to another, gifts of healing by the one Spirit, ¹⁰to another, the performing of miracles, to another, prophecy, to another, distinguishing between spirits, to another, different kinds of languages, to another, interpretation of languages. ¹¹ But one and the same Spirit is active in all these, distributing to each person as He wills." (1 Cor. 12:4-11, HCSB)

It aids our understanding to categorize spiritual gifts described in the Scripture.

"…And there are different activities, but the same God activates each gift in each person." (1 Cor. 12:6, HCSB)

These gifts are used by God to shape a believer's perspective on life and motivate his words and actions. Romans 12:3-8 illuminates our understanding. We are all one body made up of different parts that function differently with the gifts given to us by grace. These gifts cause us to "Arise and shake ourselves from the dust," as instructed in Isaiah 52:2. They cause us to tread unchartered territory that God has marked for us. It basically motivates us to do what we would otherwise not even attempt.

MOTIVATIONAL GIFTS

"⁶According to the grace given to us, we have different gifts: If prophecy, use it according to the standard of one's faith; ⁷ if service, in service; if teaching, in teaching; ⁸ if exhorting, in exhortation; giving, with generosity; leading, with diligence; showing mercy, with cheerfulness. (Rom. 12:6-8, HCSB)

1. Prophecy
2. Ministry/Serving
3. Teaching
4. Encouraging
5. Giving
6. Organizing/Leadership/Governing
7. Mercy

MINISTRY GIFTS

"There are different ministries, but the same Lord." (1 Cor. 12:5, HCSB)

This is how God works through a believer to serve and meet the needs of others. Ephesians 4:11–15 and 1 Corinthians 12:27–31 serve as a good reference point. Ministry Gifts are the gifts given to some Christians to hold a specific office in the church. This is not given to all believers. What is the purpose of the ministry gifts?

[11] "And He personally gave some to be apostles, some prophets, some evangelists, some pastors and teachers, [12] for the training of the saints in the work of ministry, to build up the body of Christ, [13] until we all reach unity in the faith and in the knowledge of God's Son, growing into a mature man with a stature measured by Christ's fullness." (Eph. 4:11-13, HCSB)

"[28] And God has placed these in the church: first apostles, second prophets, third teachers, next miracles, then gifts of healing, helping, managing, various kinds of languages. [29] Are all apostles? Are all prophets? Are all teachers? Do all do miracles? [30] Do all have gifts of healing? Do all speak in other languages? Do all interpret?" (1 Cor. 12:28-30, HCSB)

In this passage, Paul is not referring to the manifestation gifts. He is referring to gifts of office mentioned above – apostles, prophets, evangelists, pastors, and teachers. These verses are often quoted to disprove the manifestation of the gifts of the Spirit. The gift of ministry must not be mixed up with the manifestation gift.

For instance, while every Christian is urged to desire to prophesy, not everyone is a prophet. All believers may speak in tongues to edify themselves - not everyone has to speak out loud in church and interpret. In this passage, it is easy to mix up the ministry of speaking in tongues (to edify the church) with the personal gift of tongues (to edify the individual). Additionally, not everyone is called to be a pastor or apostle. This is the context of these verses.

MANIFESTATION GIFTS

"A demonstration of the Spirit is given to each person to produce what is beneficial..." (1 Cor. 12:7, HCSB)

These gifts manifest God's presence and might. These gifts leave no doubt about God's omnipotence. God uses all of the gifts in each of these three categories to minister to His Church and to accomplish His work in the world. Each believer uses the gifts and comes together as the united body of Christ. Each member is different, but necessary.

MANIFESTATION GIFTS

Categories of Spiritual Gifts

Revelation	Power	Utterance
Word of knowledge	Faith	Prophecy
Word of wisdom	Working of miracles	Diverse tongues
Discerning of spirits	Gifts of healings	Interpretation of tongues

WORD OF KNOWLEDGE

> "...to one is given a message of wisdom through the Spirit, to another, a message of knowledge by the same Spirit..." (1 Cor. 12:8, HCSB)

God knows everything but does not reveal everything to man. He just gives us a word or a fragment of knowledge that we need to know. This is not natural knowledge, but supernatural knowledge, revealing facts about the past or present, but not the future.

Ananias

> ""Get up and go to the street called Straight," the Lord said to him, "to the house of Judas, and ask for a man from Tarsus named Saul, since he is praying there.""
> (Acts 9:11, HCSB)

Ananias was given clear details about Saul's location. God was revealing all the exact names and places needed for Ananias to minister effectively to Saul.

Elisha's Servant

> "Then Elisha prayed, "Lord, please open his eyes and let him see." So the Lord opened the servant's eyes. He looked and saw that the mountain was covered with horses and chariots of fire all around Elisha." (2 Kings 6:17, HCSB)

Here the spiritual facts have been revealed to the servant through a vision. Elisha was praying that his spiritual eyes would be opened. The word of knowledge and word of wisdom can be conveyed through dreams, visions, or just the words of man's mouth.

Ananias and Saphira

> "Then Peter said, "Ananias, why has Satan filled your heart to lie to the Holy Spirit and keep back part of the proceeds from the field?"" (Acts 5:3, HCSB)

The fact that Ananias and his wife Sapphira hid a portion of money was not known to anybody. God revealed it to Peter through the Spirit.

WORD OF WISDOM

A word of wisdom is a supernatural revelation from God about our situation. The Holy Spirit reveals the divine purpose and will of God to us. The word is only a fragment of God's will. This may apply to the future, unlike the Word of knowledge that deals with present or past facts. This gift is prophetic in nature and is easily mistaken for prophecy. Sometimes, the word of knowledge and the word of wisdom operate together. This can be communicated through dreams, visions, and a word through a believer.

Pharaoh's Dreams

In Genesis 41, Pharaoh had a dream, but Joseph interpreted the meaning of the 'word' that God had for Pharaoh. Since Pharaoh was the ruler, God was warning him of things to come so that preparations could be made.

> "It is just as I told Pharaoh: God has shown Pharaoh what He is about to do." (Gen. 41:28, HCSB)

Not only was the future problem foretold, God gave Joseph the wisdom to present a solution that would save Egypt and Jacob's family. The plan was to save a fifth of the grain for the years of famine.

Samuel Meets Saul

> "15 Now the day before Saul's arrival, the Lord had informed Samuel, 16 "At this time tomorrow I will send you a man from the land of Benjamin. Anoint him ruler over My people Israel. He will save them from the hand of the Philistines because I have seen the affliction of My people, for their cry has come to Me." (1 Sam. 9:15-16, HCSB)

DISCERNING OF SPIRITS

The gift of discerning of spirits gives us insight into the spirit world. Its revelation is limited to a single class – spirits. This is not just a gift to discern evil spirits, but it is supernatural insight into the spirit realm. This also includes discerning of cherubim, seraphim, hosts of angels, Satan, and demons. It also refers to discerning of the human spirit and its good and evil tendencies.

Several instances can be seen across the Bible – John's vision of Jesus at Patmos (Rev. 1), John's vision of the sevenfold Spirit before the throne of God (Rev. 4:5), and Isaiah's vision of the Lord upon His throne (Isa. 6, HCSB).

Paul and The Fortune-Teller

Paul identifying a demon hiding under the guise of a good person (Acts 16:16-18, HCSB).

> "¹⁶ Once, as we were on our way to prayer, a slave girl met us who had a spirit of prediction. She made a large profit for her owners by fortune-telling. ¹⁷ As she followed Paul and us she cried out, "These men, who are proclaiming to you the way of salvation, are the slaves of the Most High God." ¹⁸ And she did this for many days. But Paul was greatly aggravated and turning to the spirit, said, "I command you in the name of Jesus Christ to come out of her!" And it came out right away""
> (Acts 16:16-18, HCSB)

Paul was able to tell that this was a demon, even though she was speaking 'Christianese'. This revelation was given to Paul by the Holy Spirit.

PROPHECY

> "But he that prophesieth speaketh unto men to edification, and exhortation, and comfort." (1 Cor. 14:3, KJV)

The word 'edify' means to instruct, benefit, or uplift, especially morally or spiritually. The word 'exhort' represents the action to urge, advise, or caution earnestly, admonish urgently, to give urgent advice, recommendations, or warnings. The word 'comfort' represents any address, whether made for the purpose of persuading, or of arousing and stimulating, or of calming and consoling.

One could understand forthtelling to mean to speak forth what God has revealed. Another purpose for forthtelling prophecy is to give instruction. Instruction through forthtelling happens when God is telling someone to live in a certain way or to do something.

> "Pursue love and desire spiritual gifts, and above all that you may prophesy."
> (1 Cor. 14:1, HCSB)

> "Therefore, my brothers, be eager to prophesy, and do not forbid speaking in other languages." (1 Cor. 14:39, HCSB)

The Bible says in 1 Corinthians 14:5 that the person who prophesies is greater than the person who speaks in languages, even though both are inspired utterances. Tongues, of course, are inspired utterances in an unknown or foreign tongue. The interpretation of tongues is inspired utterance telling that which was spoken in tongues. Prophecy, on the other hand, is inspired utterance in a known or familiar tongue.

> "I wish all of you spoke in other languages, but even more that you prophesied. The person who prophesies is greater than the person who speaks in languages, unless he interprets so that the church may be built up." (1 Cor. 14:5, HCSB)

This verse approximates prophecy to be an amalgamation of tongues and their interpretation.

Saul and Barnabus

In Acts 13:1-3 the Holy Spirit specifically instructs for Paul and Barnabas to be set aside for ministry purposes.

Samuel

Samuel tells Saul the message from God for Saul to destroy all of the Amalekites (1 Sam. 15:1-3). The instruction from God was specific - for Saul to kill everyone and everything.

Agabus

> "²⁷In those days some prophets came down from Jerusalem to Antioch. ²⁸Then one of them, named Agabus, stood up and predicted by the Spirit that there would be a severe famine throughout the Roman world. This took place during the time of Claudius. ²⁹So each of the disciples, according to his ability, determined to send relief to the brothers who lived in Judea." (Acts 11:27-29, HCSB)

He who prophesies must do in proportion to his faith. Prophecy must be done in the fear of the Lord. If we speak our own words in the Name of the Lord, we will be held accountable to the Lord.

In the Old Testament, a prophet was proven by the fact that what he foretold would come to pass. If his prophecy was not fulfilled, he would be stoned.

A False Prophet and A Real One

Hananiah was a popular false prophet. He prophesied to the priests and people in the temple. Jeremiah 28:2-4 tells us the story about Hananiah who spoke words that made the people feel better. God was going to send the Jews into captivity, but Hananiah spoke otherwise. He broke a yoke in front of the court proclaiming that in the same manner the yoke of Babylon would be broken, and that all the stolen treasures would be returned in two years. King Jeconiah would be restored and the exiles brought back to their homeland. He spoke vain words in the name of the Lord. Hananiah broke the yoke on Jeremiah's neck and said that God would break the yoke of Babylon. Now we see why he was so popular. He spoke what people wanted to hear, not what was true.

"¹²The word of the Lord came to Jeremiah after Hananiah the prophet had broken the yoke bar from the neck of Jeremiah the prophet: ¹³"Go say to Hananiah: This is what the Lord says, 'You broke a wooden yoke bar, but in its place you will make an iron yoke bar.' ¹⁴For this is what the Lord of Hosts, the God of Israel, says, 'I have put an iron yoke on the neck of all these nations that they might serve King Nebuchadnezzar of Babylon, and they will serve him. I have also put the wild animals under him.'" ¹⁵The prophet Jeremiah said to the prophet Hananiah, "Listen, Hananiah! The Lord did not send you, but you have led these people to trust in a lie. ¹⁶Therefore, this is what the Lord says: 'I am about to send you off the face of the earth. You will die this year because you have spoken rebellion against the Lord.'" (Jer. 28:12-16, HCSB)

Every word that Jeremiah spoke came to pass. Verse 17 commends Jeremiah's prediction and tells us what happened to the prophet Hananiah.

"And the prophet Hananiah died that year in the seventh month." (Jer. 28:17, HCSB)

DIVERSE TONGUES

There are two types of usage for the gift of tongues. One is a personal gift to speak to God as a prayer language. The other is the gift of tongues to communicate God's message to the whole church. In 1 Corinthians 14: 12-40, Paul discusses the difference between the public and private use of tongues. The public gift of tongues is different from the personal gift.

> "[18] I thank God that I speak in other languages more than all of you; [19] yet in the church I would rather speak five words with my understanding, in order to teach others also, than 10,000 words in another language." (1 Cor. 14:18-19, HCSB)

PERSONAL GIFT OF TONGUES

> "[2] For the person who speaks in another language is not speaking to men but to God, since no one understands him; however, he speaks mysteries in the Spirit. [3] But the person who prophesies speaks to people for edification, encouragement, and consolation. [4] The person who speaks in another language builds himself up, but he who prophesies builds up the church." (1 Cor. 14:2-4, HCSB)

> "For if I pray in another language, my spirit prays, but my understanding is unfruitful." (1 Cor. 14:14, HCSB)

A believer speaks in tongues when the Holy Spirit gives him utterance. The person can experience this only when his or her spirit is yielded to the Holy Ghost

When the disciples were filled with the Spirit in Acts 2, they all spoke in tongues, declaring the great works of God.

"Then they were all filled with the Holy Spirit and began to speak in different languages, as the Spirit gave them ability for speech." (Acts 2:4, HCSB)

> "[6] When this sound occurred, a crowd came together and was confused because each one heard them speaking in his own language. [7] And they were astounded and amazed..." (Acts 2:6-7, HCSB)

> "...we hear them speaking the magnificent acts of God in our own languages." (Acts 2:11, HCSB)

This is an example of men speaking in tongues of men. There are also tongues that no man can understand.

Purpose of the personal gift of tongues

The object of the two types of tongues is the same, to speak forth the wonderful works of God. The spirit of the man and the Holy Spirit are in the closest communion. The Holy Spirit transfers revelation of Christ and understanding of mysteries into our spirit as we pray in tongues. This supernatural knowledge brings us out of troubles, hindrances, and even brings change to our flawed character. The gift of tongues must never be misused to bring glory to oneself. It is always meant to bring glory to God.

Edification

"The person who speaks in another language builds himself up, but he who prophesies builds up the church." (1 Cor. 14: 4, HCSB)

"But you, dear friends, as you build yourselves up in your most holy faith and pray in the Holy Spirit" (Jude 1:20, HCSB)

The word 'edify' means to build yourself up from the foundation; to restore by building, to rebuild, repair; to found, establish; or to promote growth in Christian wisdom, affection, grace, virtue, holiness, and blessedness. Our spirit is like a building. It is founded on faith, and the edifice is built up by praying in the Holy Ghost. As we continue to pray, we draw strength for our spirit. Praying in tongues prepares our spirits to receive revelation from the Word. The combination of tongues and the Word brings nourishment to our spirit. When this happens, the believer experiences spiritual growth.

Rest and Refreshment

"He had said to them: "This is the place of rest, let the weary rest; this is the place of repose." ..." (Isa. 28:12, HCSB)

We get rest and refreshment when we pray in the Spirit. All weariness will vanish in His presence. When our Spirit is refreshed, His life will flow from our spirt to our soul and body.

"For if I pray in another language, my spirit prays, but my understanding is unfruitful." (1 Cor. 14:14, HCSB)

When we pray in tongues, the Holy Spirit bypasses our understanding and communicates revelation and mysteries directly to our spirit. This does not mean that God wants us to be mindless followers. We are simply allowing our spirit to take the lead with our mind following in subjection. We are a spirit being, and our spirits need refreshing, just as our minds need renewing.

TONGUES AND INTERPRETATION

GIFT OF TONGUES

I believe God desires every believer to speak to Him in tongues. For now, we will focus on the use of the gift in church. The gift of tongues is used when God wants to convey a message to the body. God decides to speak through a person or two to the whole congregation. One must speak at a time while others listen.

Purpose of public gift of tongues

"⁶ But now, brothers, if I come to you speaking in other languages, how will I benefit you unless I speak to you with a revelation or knowledge or prophecy or teaching? ⁷ Even inanimate things that produce sounds – whether flute or harp – if they don't make a distinction in the notes, how will what is played on the flute or harp be recognized? ⁸ In fact, if the trumpet makes an unclear sound, who will prepare for battle?" (1 Cor. 14:6-8, HCSB)

Verse 6 mentions revelation, knowledge, prophecy, and instruction, while verses 7 and 8 state that the message must be distinct and clear, complete with meaning.

Public use of the gift of tongues

When in public, keep in mind that God desires to edify the church.

"Therefore the person who speaks in another language should pray that he can interpret." (1 Cor. 14:13, HCSB)

If you are unable to interpret your message in tongues, then it is better to speak quietly to yourself.

"But if there is no interpreter, that person should keep silent in the church and speak to himself and to God." (1 Cor. 14:28, HCSB)

"It follows that speaking in other languages is intended as a sign, not for believers but for unbelievers. But prophecy is not for unbelievers but for believers." (1 Cor. 14:22, HCSB)

"Therefore, if the whole church assembles together and all are speaking in other languages and people who are uninformed or unbelievers come in, will they not say that you are out of your minds?" (1 Cor. 14:23, HCSB)

Tongues are a sign to unbelievers only when coupled with interpretation. Otherwise it is mere gibberish to an outsider, as stated in verse 23.

One at a time

"And the prophets' spirits are under the control of the prophets..." (1 Cor. 14:32, HCSB)

Prophesy in turn, and so order will be maintained. This way, we honor the presence of God. God is a God of order. Nobody must be disruptive.

"...since God is not a God of disorder but of peace." (1 Cor. 14:33, HCSB)

POWER GIFTS

GIFT OF FAITH

"Faith - not of doctrines, but of miracles: confidence in God, by the impulse of His Spirit, that He would enable them to perform any required miracle." (Jamieson, Fausset & Brown)[2]

This is different from saving faith, though it operates the same way. This is not the faith that comes by hearing the word that grows as we pray. The gift of faith is in operation when the believer has a great unction of the Spirit that results in a miracle. This is faith that moves mountains. This great faith was put into effect when Moses lifted the rod and God parted the Red Sea.

The Day the Sun Stood Still

Remember how Joshua spoke through the Lord and the sun stood still?

"[12] On the day the Lord gave the Amorites over to the Israelites, Joshua spoke to the Lord in the presence of Israel: "Sun, stand still over Gibeon, and moon, over the Valley of Aijalon." [13] And the sun stood still and the moon stopped until the nation took vengeance on its enemies. Isn't this written in the Book of Jashar? So the sun stopped in the middle of the sky and delayed its setting almost a full day. [14] There has been no day like it before or since, when the Lord listened to the voice of a man, because the Lord fought for Israel." (Josh. 10:12-14, HCSB)

GIFTS OF HEALINGS

Healing is supposed to flow through every believer, but this gift rests upon certain people in a special way. Their ministry is characterized by unusual healings. They operate in an atmosphere of healing.

Peter's shadow

"As a result, they would carry the sick out into the streets and lay them on cots and mats so that when Peter came by, at least his shadow might fall on some of them." (Acts 5:15, HCSB)

Aeneas

"[32] As Peter was traveling from place to place, he also came down to the saints who lived in Lydda. [33] There he found a man named Aeneas, who was paralyzed and had been bedridden for eight years. [34] Peter said to him, "Aeneas, Jesus Christ heals you.

Get up and make your bed," and immediately he got up. ³⁵So all who lived in Lydda and Sharon saw him and turned to the Lord." (Acts 9: 32-35, HCSB)

This is the purpose of this gift. People respond to supernatural healing. They cannot deny the power of the Lord to heal because it produces tangible results.

WORKING OF MIRACLES

All healings are miracles; hence this must refer to miracles of special and extraordinary power. The Greek word for miracles is *dunamis*, which means power. This is from where we derive the word 'dynamite.' This gift displays God's power. It is a supernatural manifestation that changes, lays aside, or controls the laws of nature.

Examples of miracles – the raising of Dorcas from the dead by Peter (Acts 9:36-42); Paul's recovery from a snake bite (Acts 28:3-5); Water changing to wine (John 2); and the floating of Elijah's axe head (2 Kings 6:1-7).

Even in Acts 19:11-12, God performed extraordinary miracles through Paul, so that when handkerchiefs and aprons that had touched him were taken to the sick, their illnesses were cured and the evil spirits left them.

SECTION 9
TEMPLE OF THE HOLY SPIRIT

GOD DWELLING WITH MAN

"They are to make a sanctuary for Me so that I may dwell among them."
(Ex. 25:8, HCSB)

God wanted to dwell in the midst of the Israeli camp in the wilderness. He wanted to 'camp' with them. I don't know about you, but I only go camping with people I like. I think God 'likes' us. It just blows my mind that He would desire to be with us all the time.

The New Testament tells us that we are the temple of the Holy Ghost. It is therefore fitting to look at all the shadows of the Tabernacle and Temple and draw parallels to our lives.

THE TABERNACLE

The Tabernacle is also called the 'Tent of Meeting'. It was a portable tent where God was worshipped while Israel was in the Wilderness. It was in the center of the camps. Exodus 40:1-8 gives a detailed description of the layout.

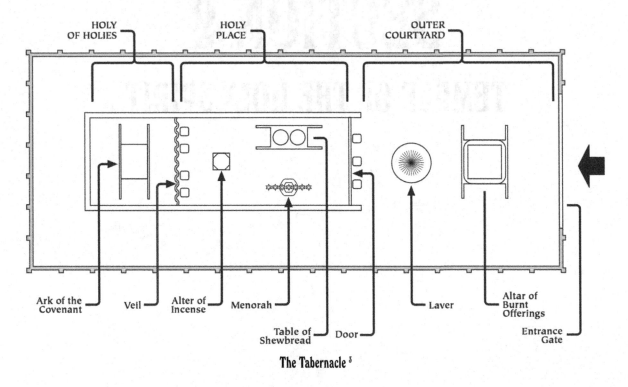

The Tabernacle [3]

PARTS OF THE TABERNACLE

The layout of the Tabernacle can be divided into two parts – the Tent and the external court. The court was made up of a high fence with only one entrance called the Gate. The Tent was divided into two sections by the Veil – the Holy Place and the Most Holy Place (Holy of Holies).

Sections of the Tabernacle

OUTER COURT	HOLY PLACE	HOLY OF HOLIES
Gate	Table of shewbread	
Brazen altar	Candlestick	Ark of the covenant
Laver	Altar of incense	

The words *Naos* and *Skene* are used to describe the dwelling of God with man throughout scripture. *Naos* refers to the Holy Place or Sanctuary and *Skene* to the tent.

The theme of the Tabernacle and God's dwelling with man is seen throughout scripture. Did you know that God wants to dwell (*skenoo*) with you? As we walk through scripture, we see this as a recurring theme. God wants to go camping with us. Actually, He wants to dwell right in the midst of our camp and inhabit His sanctuary in our innermost being. Let us pursue this theme through the pages of scripture.

ISRAEL

> "45 I will dwell among the Israelites and be their God. 46 And they will know that I am Yahweh their God, who brought them out of the land of Egypt, so that I might dwell among them. I am Yahweh their God." (Ex. 29:45-46, HCSB)

Moses was instructed to build this worldly sanctuary according to the pattern of the perfect, heavenly sanctuary in heaven.

> "You must make it according to all that I show you – the pattern of the tabernacle as well as the pattern of all its furnishings." (Ex. 25: 9, HCSB)

This Tabernacle in the wilderness was an earthly model (*parabola*) of the one in heaven. It is like a model car your children would have. It looks just like the real thing. When they look at the model car, they can see the real thing in their mind's eye. They can play with it and even imagine themselves driving down the highway. It is as close as they can come to the real thing as a child! However, it is not anywhere close to experiencing the real thing.

JESUS

> "The Word became flesh and took up residence among us. We observed His glory, the glory as the One and Only Son from the Father, full of grace and truth." (John 1:14, HCSB)

The Living Word, Jesus Christ dwelt (*skenoo*) with us. Jesus fulfilled the design of the Tabernacle by coming and camping with men in the flesh. When Jesus became man, His tabernacle was His flesh. It just blows my mind that Jesus took on the form of a man (His earthly tent) and camped among us. How much further can one reach out to a fallen race? Oh! The extent of the mercy of God!

BELIEVERS

> "Jesus answered, "If anyone loves Me, he will keep My word. My Father will love him, and We will come to him and make Our home with him." (John 14:23, HCSB)

> "Don't you know that your body is a sanctuary of the Holy Spirit who is in you, whom you have from God? You are not your own..." (1 Cor. 6:19, HCSB)

What an honor it is to be chosen to be the temples of the Holy Ghost! The High and Lofty One who inhabits eternity yearns to take up residence in the spirit of the contrite believer.

HEAVEN

> "God's sanctuary in heaven was opened, and the ark of His covenant appeared in His sanctuary..." (Rev. 11:19a, HCSB)

The *naos* of the *skene* indicated the Holy Place or Sanctuary of the tent. The sanctuary is referred to as *naos* and the Tabernacle as *skene*. The word *naos* is used of the sacred edifice (sanctuary) itself, which consisted of the Holy Place and the Holy of Holies.

> "And after that I looked, and, behold, the temple of the tabernacle of the testimony in heaven was opened." (Rev. 15:5, KJV)

Why is there a Temple in heaven? This Tabernacle also had a Most Holy Place which Jesus entered through the Veil, making the Way open for us through the blood of Jesus. Moses saw this *naos* and was instructed to fashion the earthly Tabernacle like this one.

> "Then the sanctuary was filled with smoke from God's glory and from His power, and no one could enter the sanctuary..." (Rev. 15:8, HCSB)

The Temple is full of His glory. Can you imagine that His glory dwells in us?

"Then I heard a loud voice from the throne: Look! God's dwelling is with humanity, and He will live with them. They will be His people, and God Himself will be with them and be their God." (Rev. 21:3, HCSB)

"I did not see a sanctuary in it, because the Lord God the Almighty and the Lamb are its sanctuary." (Rev. 21:22, HCSB)

There is no Temple seen in Revelation 21, as God will then be dwelling in the midst of His people in New Jerusalem. This is the ultimate fulfillment of God's plan of dwelling with man, originally revealed in the figure of the Tabernacle and Temple, fulfilled in Christ and reaching perfection in eternity in heaven.

SOLOMON'S TEMPLE

WHO BUILT IT?

David desired to build the Temple, but God did not allow this as David was a man of war and had shed much blood. Instead, his son Solomon was granted the responsibility of building the Temple. David prepared abundantly before his death.

> "Then David said, "This is the house of the Lord God, and this is the altar of burnt offering for Israel." ²So David gave orders to gather the foreigners that were in the land of Israel, and he appointed stonecutters to cut finished stones for building God's house. ³David supplied a great deal of iron to make the nails for the doors of the gateways and for the fittings, together with an immeasurable quantity of bronze, ⁴and innumerable cedar logs because the Sidonians and Tyrians had brought a large quantity of cedar logs to David. ⁵David said, "My son Solomon is young and inexperienced, and the house that is to be built for the Lord must be exceedingly great and famous and glorious in all the lands. Therefore, I must make provision for it." So David made lavish preparations for it before his death." (1 Chron. 22:1-5, HCSB)

PATTERN

> "¹¹Then David gave his son Solomon the plans for the portico of the temple and its buildings, treasuries, upper rooms, inner rooms, and a room for the mercy seat. ¹² The plans contained everything he had in mind for the courts of the Lord's house, all the surrounding chambers, the treasuries of God's house, and the treasuries for what is dedicated." (1 Chron. 28:11-12, HCSB)

The layout of the Temple was very similar to the Tabernacle, though the temple furniture was made on a grander scale. Gold symbolized divinity and the bronze symbolized humanity. All the articles of bronze, such as the brazen altar of sacrifice and the Laver, deal with our flesh. All the golden objects point us to His divinity and are dedicated to His worship alone.

LOCATION

The Temple was located on Mt. Moriah on the threshing floor of Ornan the Jebusite.

CHERUBIM

In the Temple, the cherubim were engraved on the walls and they were woven into the Veil. Two massive cherubim were in the Holy of Holies overshadowing the Ark. They were overlaid with gold and their wings were outstretched. The combined wingspan of both cherubim filled the whole room and was 20 cubits in length. Do not forget the two smaller cherubim above the Mercy Seat. Why were there such a profusion of cherubim? They were an indicator that the worshipper was moving closer to the Presence. The cherubim are the guardians or sentinels before the throne of God.

PILLARS

Two brass pillars were crafted 18 cubits high in the porch of the Temple. One pillar was named *Jachin*, meaning 'Yah will establish', and the second pillar was named *Boaz*, which means 'in its strength'. *Boaz* was to the left when entering Solomon's Temple, while *Jachin* was to the right. The brass element refers to humanity.

When God desired to build the Temple, God promised David a 'house' and a 'throne'. The pillars represent the fact that God would bring the messianic line and government through two men – David and Solomon.

Jesus was a descendant of Solomon (right to throne) and a descendant of Nathan (Davidic lineage). Both Mary and Joseph descended from Nathan and Solomon. Through both his parents, Jesus inherited the 'house' and the 'throne'. The brass capitals were adorned with pomegranates which represent the seed of David and Solomon. These pillars show that God brings His promises to pass in the lives of men. He is sovereign and establishes His covenant in strength.

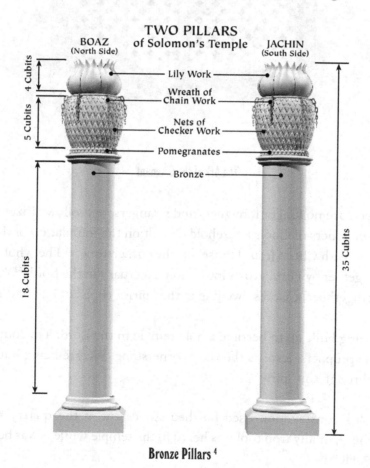

Bronze Pillars [4]

2 Chronicles 3 describes Solomon's Temple for the Lord. Built on Mt. Moriah in the city of Jerusalem, the Temple was constructed on the threshing floor of Ornan the Jebusite. It took seven years to complete the construction of the Temple.

CONSTRUCTION

The Temple was made of stone, paneled with wood, and overlaid with gold. 1 Kings 6:18 specifies that not a stone could be seen. This picture of the gold overlaying the wood and stone is a symbol of Christ covering our weaknesses. The Temple was made of stone, but no stone was visible. Likewise, when God looks at us (His temple), He sees us in the righteousness of Christ.

The Ark of the Covenant

"[19]So then you are no longer foreigners and strangers, but fellow citizens with the saints, and members of God's household, [20]built on the foundation of the apostles and prophets, with Christ Jesus Himself as the cornerstone. [21]The whole building, being put together by Him, grows into a holy sanctuary in the Lord. [22]You also are being built together for God's dwelling in the Spirit." (Eph. 2:19-22, HCSB)

We are all stones being built up to become a holy temple in the Lord. The foundation is made of the apostles and the prophets. Jesus is the chief cornerstone. We are being built together for the habitation of God through the Spirit.

"The temple's construction used finished stones cut at the quarry so that no hammer, chisel, or any iron tool was heard in the temple while it was being built." (1 Kings 6:7, HCSB)

This verse implies that we are each being quarried and chiseled independently. We are all being prepared or made ready where no one can see us. It may make you uncomfortable during the time of chiseling, but it is all part of God's grand design. The building of Solomon's Temple was a smooth process. This is typical of the Kingdom of God, which grows quickly but without much ado. For example, in the parables of the mustard seed and the yeast, individually the mustard seed and the yeast seem insignificant at first, but over time the seed grows and becomes a huge tree, and the yeast spreads throughout the whole dough.

THE BRAZEN ALTAR

> "⁶Then one of the seraphim flew to me, and in his hand was a glowing coal that he had taken from the altar with tongs. ⁷ He touched my mouth with it and said: Now that this has touched your lips, your wickedness is removed and your sin is atoned for." (Isa. 6:6-7, HCSB)

The Altar is a place of death, blood, and fire. The coals from the Altar of Sacrifice were taken to the Altar of Incense. It is the blood on the coals that is significant. It is a place of atonement by substitution. This also points directly to the Cross and the sacrifice of Jesus on our behalf for the remission of sins.

> "For the life of a creature is in the blood, and I have appointed it to you to make atonement on the altar for your lives, since it is the lifeblood that makes atonement." (Lev. 17:11, HCSB)

We have to deal with the humanity of our sinful flesh before we enter the Holiest Place. Only once our sin is atoned for with the shed blood of a sacrificed lamb can we enter in to commune with God.

THE SEA

The Sea was a much grander version of the Laver from the Tabernacle. It was a huge brazen vessel. The priests most likely washed in the ten smaller lavers.

THE LAVER

The Laver, made of bronze and mirrors, was only used by the priests. It was where the priests washed their hands and feet of the filth related to sacrifice before they ministered inside the Tent. The priests died if they did not wash at the Laver. When the priest bent over to wash in the Laver, he would peer into the Laver and see his reflection. In this mirror, any spots or dirt were clearly seen for the priest to wash it off.

> "We all, with unveiled faces, are looking as in a mirror at the glory of the Lord and are being transformed into the same image from glory to glory; this is from the Lord who is the Spirit." (2 Cor. 3:18, HCSB)

This is a representation of us as priests being cleansed as we look into the mirror of the Word. It highlights all our flaws and we are changed into His likeness as we gaze upon His beauty.

TABLE OF SHEWBREAD

> "Take fine flour and bake it into 12 loaves; each loaf is to be made with four quarts." (Lev. 24:5, HCSB)

The shewbread (bread of the Presence) was comprised of unleavened bread. There was a loaf for each tribe.

> "6 Arrange them in two rows, six to a row, on the pure gold table before the Lord. 7 Place pure frankincense near each row, so that it may serve as a memorial portion for the bread and a fire offering to the Lord. 8 The bread is to be set out before the Lord every Sabbath day as a perpetual covenant obligation on the part of the Israelites." (Lev. 24:6-8, HCSB)

The loaves were changed once a week on the Sabbath.

> "It belongs to Aaron and his sons, who are to eat it in a holy place, for it is the holiest portion for him from the fire offerings to the Lord; this is a permanent rule." (Lev. 24:9, HCSB)

The bread represents spiritual food, and ultimately, that Jesus is the Bread of Life.

THE CANDLESTICK

The Candlestick was made of pure gold. It had seven lamps with wicks that needed trimming every day. The oil in the lamps needed to be replenished in the morning and evening. The light of the Candlesticks was never to go out. The light within us is fueled by the anointing or 'oil' of the Holy Ghost.

ALTAR OF INCENSE

The altar was a smaller version of the altar of sacrifice. They were both made of acacia wood. The difference is that the altar of incense was overlaid with gold, while the altar of sacrifice was overlaid with bronze. The gold signifies that the worshipper is no longer looking at himself, but is offering prayer and worship focused on God.

Purpose and Function

> "7 Aaron must burn fragrant incense on it; he must burn it every morning when he tends the lamps. 8 When Aaron sets up the lamps at twilight, he must burn incense.

There is to be an incense offering before the Lord throughout your generations. (Ex. 30:7, HCSB)

"³ Another angel, with a gold incense burner, came and stood at the altar. He was given a large amount of incense to offer with the prayers of all the saints on the gold altar in front of the throne. ⁴ The smoke of the incense, with the prayers of the saints, went up in the presence of God from the angel's hand." (Rev. 8:3-4, HCSB)

The incense that is offered on the altar represents prayer going up to God. This is a shadow of God desiring His people to be in prayer (communion, fellowship with God) all the time. Prayer is just communing with God.

"You must not offer unauthorized incense on it, or a burnt or grain offering; you are not to pour a drink offering on it." (Ex. 30: 9, HCSB)

God wanted no substitutes or imitations. He wants true prayer from the heart, not just a form of godliness.

"Once a year Aaron is to perform the purification rite on the horns of the altar. Throughout your generations, he is to perform the purification rite for it once a year, with the blood of the sin offering for atonement. The altar is especially holy to the Lord." (Ex. 30: 10, HCSB)

This was to happen once a year on the Day of Atonement, when the High Priest entered the Holy of Holies. If the offering of the High Priest was accepted, the whole nation was accepted. This sacrifice would tide the worshipper over till the next year. We are accepted, because our High Priest is perfect! His blood has made atonement for us once and for all.

HOLY OF HOLIES

"The interior of the sanctuary was 30 feet long, 30 feet wide, and 30 feet high; he overlaid it with pure gold. He also overlaid the cedar altar." (1 Kings 6:20, HCSB)

The Oracle's dimensions were 20 x 20 x 20 cubits and was overlaid with gold. It contained the two cherubim, which overshadowed the Ark.

THE ARK

The Ark of the Covenant consisted of two parts – the Mercy Seat and the box itself.

Characteristics of The Ark

The Ark, made of acacia or shittim wood, was overlaid with pure gold. It had four rings – one at each of the four corners. It had four staves (for transport) that remain in the rings.

The Mercy Seat

The Mercy Seat had a lid molded out of a single piece of pure gold. There were two cherubim on top facing each other looking towards the Mercy Seat. It was here that the blood was sprinkled by the High Priest and God would speak to His people.

Significance

> "Set the mercy seat on top of the ark and put the testimony that I will give you into the ark." (Ex. 25:21, HCSB)

The mercy seat is over the tablets of stone. The Ten Commandments talk of judgment and condemnation. It signifies that mercy has triumphed over judgment.

> "I will meet with you there above the mercy seat, between the two cherubim that are over the ark of the testimony..." (Ex. 25:22, HCSB)

This is what is important about the mercy seat. It is the place from which God chose to speak intimately with His people. God and Adam used to commune every day. This was destroyed by sin, and restored by the atoning blood on the mercy seat.

> "20For no one will be justified in His sight by the works of the law, because the knowledge of sin comes through the law. 21 But now, apart from the law, God's righteousness has been revealed – attested by the Law and the Prophets" (Rom. 3:20-21, HCSB)

This is the righteousness that comes from not just doing the works of the law, but by grace through faith in Jesus.

> "24 They are justified freely by His grace through the redemption that is in Christ Jesus. 25 God presented Him as a propitiation through faith in His blood, to demonstrate His righteousness, because in His restraint God passed over the sins previously committed." (Rom. 3:24-25, HCSB)

The mercy seat is Jesus and in Him is atonement, forgiveness and righteousness.

TEMPLE DEDICATION

The Temple of Solomon was dedicated with great honor and reverence. All the men were present to honor Jehovah. No lame excuses were made to avoid this occasion. Observe the lavish sacrifices and devotion of His people. What would happen if we took time out of our schedules and devoted ourselves to Him?

> "² At that time Solomon assembled at Jerusalem the elders of Israel – all the tribal heads, the ancestral chiefs of the Israelites – in order to bring the ark of the covenant of the Lord up from the city of David, that is, Zion. ³ So all the men of Israel were assembled in the king's presence at the festival; this was in the seventh month.⁴ All the elders of Israel came, and the Levites picked up the ark. ⁵ They brought up the ark, the tent of meeting, and the holy utensils that were in the tent. The priests and the Levites brought them up. ⁶ King Solomon and the entire congregation of Israel who had gathered around him were in front of the ark sacrificing sheep and cattle that could not be counted or numbered because there were so many. ⁷ The priests brought the ark of the Lord's covenant to its place, into the inner sanctuary of the temple, to the most holy place, beneath the wings of the cherubim."
> (2 Chron. 5:2-7, HCSB)

They had learnt from the story of Uzzah, and everything was done according to God's order. The Levites carried the Ark and laid it in its resting place.

> "¹² ...the Levitical singers dressed in fine linen and carrying cymbals, harps, and lyres were standing east of the altar, and with them were 120 priests blowing trumpets. The Levitical singers were descendants of Asaph, Heman, and Jeduthun and their sons and relatives. ¹³ The trumpeters and singers joined together to praise and thank the Lord with one voice. They raised their voices, accompanied by trumpets, cymbals, and musical instruments, in praise to the Lord : For He is good; His faithful love endures forever. The temple, the Lord's temple, was filled with a cloud. ¹⁴ And because of the cloud, the priests were not able to continue ministering, for the glory of the Lord filled God's temple." (2 Chron. 5:12-14, HCSB)

This is an Old Testament shadow of the outpouring of the Holy Spirit. There were 120 believers in one accord in the upper room in Acts 2. There is a pattern here. If we seek His face and invite Him into our hearts, will He not respond to us? Will He not fill those who hunger and thirst for His Presence?

SOLOMON'S PRAYER

"But will God indeed live on earth with man? Even heaven, the highest heaven, cannot contain You, much less this temple I have built." (2 Chron. 6:18, HCSB)

This is a great question. The heavens aren't big enough for Him. This minuscule temple seems ridiculous in comparison. Is it even possible for God to dwell in something so small?

"⁴⁰Now, my God, please let Your eyes be open and Your ears attentive to the prayer of this place. ⁴¹ Now therefore: Arise, Lord God, come to Your resting place, You and Your powerful ark..." (2 Chron. 6:40-41, HCSB)

Throughout the ages, it has been God's desire to dwell with man. If we give Him a place, He will inhabit it. The Temple was dedicated to God alone, and Solomon invited God to dwell there. God was given the due glory and reverence. He filled the house with His glory. Will you make place for God in your life today? He is longing for an invitation.

"When Solomon finished praying, fire descended from heaven and consumed the burnt offering and the sacrifices, and the glory of the Lord filled the temple." (2 Chron. 7:1, HCSB)

The priests could not enter. The people bowed themselves and offered sacrifices. There was a feast for seven whole days.

GOD'S ANSWER

"¹²Then the Lord appeared to Solomon at night and said to him: I have heard your prayer and have chosen this place for Myself as a temple of sacrifice. ¹³ If I close the sky so there is no rain, or if I command the grasshopper to consume the land, or if I send pestilence on My people, ¹⁴ and My people who are called by My name humble themselves, pray and seek My face, and turn from their evil ways, then I will hear from heaven, forgive their sin, and heal their land. ¹⁵ My eyes will now be open and My ears attentive to prayer from this place. ¹⁶And I have now chosen and consecrated this temple so that My name may be there forever; My eyes and My heart will be there at all times." (2 Chron. 7:12-16, HCSB)

Can we give God room in our lives? His eyes and heart will be upon us perpetually.

SO WHERE IS GOD'S RESTING PLACE?

Do we need to build God a fancy temple of epic proportions? Do we clean up, and only then invite Him in? All we need is a longing for Him to inhabit the very center of our being. He will take up residence and clean our deficient personalities and habits.

> "I will not allow my eyes to sleep or my eyelids to slumber ⁵ until I find a place for the Lord, a dwelling for the Mighty One of Jacob." (Ps. 132:4-5, HCSB)

Saul did not care that the Ark of God was not in the center of Israel. During his rule, it was in the outskirts of Israel, where it had remained after the Philistines captured the Ark during Eli's time. Israel lamented after the Lord. It was a pitiable state, as God was not in the center in His resting place.

As soon as David came to power, one of the first things he did was to restore the Ark to a place of rest. He did not rest till the Ark of God was given a habitation. The original tabernacle had been abandoned at Shiloh. When the Ark and the glory departed, Shiloh became a ruin. The tabernacle had lost the Ark. It was just an outer shell. The glory had departed, so how could people worship there any longer?

David was determined to find a resting place for God. He set up a tent for God in the center of Jerusalem and invited the Lord to dwell in midst of Israel. God accepted this invitation. If only we could just have David's desire! Consecrate yourself to Him. God will run to you.

> "This is what the Lord says: Heaven is My throne, and earth is My footstool. What house could you possibly build for Me? And what place could be My home? ² My hand made all these things, and so they all came into being. This is the Lord's declaration. I will look favorably on this kind of person: one who is humble, submissive in spirit, and trembles at My word." (Isa. 66:1-2, HCSB)

> "For the High and Exalted One who lives forever, whose name is Holy says this: "I live in a high and holy place, and with the oppressed and lowly of spirit, to revive the spirit of the lowly and revive the heart of the oppressed." (Isa. 57:15, HCSB)

It boggles the mind that this uncontainable God would choose to live inside this jar of clay! It looks like all we need is a large dose of humility and desire for more of God's presence.

> "Don't you yourselves know that you are God's sanctuary and that the Spirit of God lives in you?" (1 Cor. 3:16, HCSB)

SECTION 10

THE GLORY OF GOD

"The cherubim of glory were above it overshadowing the mercy seat…" (Heb. 9:5, HCSB)

"I will meet with you there above the mercy seat, between the two cherubim that are over the ark of the testimony; I will speak with you from there about all that I command you regarding the Israelites" (Ex. 25:22, HCSB)

"Listen, Shepherd of Israel…You who sit enthroned on the cherubim, rise up." (Ps. 80:1, HCSB)

ICHABOD

1 Samuel 4 elaborates how during Eli's tenure as priest in the tabernacle at Shiloh, God was not honored as He should have been. The sons of Eli did as they pleased. They were immoral and took the fat of the offering for themselves. They did not revere God, and Eli didn't restrain them from doing evil. When the Philistines attacked, the Israelites took the Ark into the battle with a great shout. The truth was that they had not given Him the glory that He was due. Just because they had the Ark with them, it did not mean that God was with them. Israel was defeated and the Ark of God was taken.

"58 They enraged Him with their high places and provoked His jealousy with their carved images. 59 God heard and became furious; He completely rejected Israel. 60 He abandoned the tabernacle at Shiloh, the tent where He resided among men. 61 He gave up His strength to captivity and His splendor to the hand of a foe." (Ps. 78:58-61, HCSB)

When Eli heard that Ark was taken he fell down and died. His sons had been killed by the Philistines. When Eli's daughter-in-law heard the news, she went into labor and bore a son. Instead of it being a time of rejoicing over her son's birth, it was a time of great sorrow. She named her son *Ichabod*, which meant 'inglorious'. The name Ichabod depicts the great desolation of Israel.

"21 She named the boy Ichabod, saying, "The glory has departed from Israel," referring to the capture of the ark of God and to the deaths of her father-in-law and her husband. 22"The glory has departed from Israel," she said, "because the ark of God has been captured."" (1 Sam. 4:21 -22, HCSB)

KABOD

The word *Kabod* is the Hebrew word used to describe the glory of God. The word implies a thick, tangible presence of God which feels like a blanket. What is the connection between the ark, the cherubim, and the Glory?

EZEKIEL'S VISION

> "I looked and there was a whirlwind coming from the north, a great cloud with fire flashing back and forth and brilliant light all around it. In the center of the fire, there was a gleam like amber." (Ezek. 1:4, HCSB)

CHERUBIM

> "5 The form of four living creatures came from it. And this was their appearance: They had human form, 6 but each of them had four faces and four wings. 7 Their legs were straight, and the soles of their feet were like the hooves of a calf, sparkling like the gleam of polished bronze. 8 They had human hands under their wings on their four sides. All four of them had faces and wings. 9 Their wings were touching. The creatures did not turn as they moved; each one went straight ahead. 10 The form of each of their faces was that of a man, and each of the four had the face of a lion on the right, the face of an ox on the left, and the face of an eagle. 11 That is what their faces were like. Their wings were spread upward; each had two wings touching that of another and two wings covering its body. 12 Each creature went straight ahead. Wherever the Spirit wanted to go, they went without turning as they moved. 13 The form of the living creatures was like the appearance of burning coals of fire and torches. Fire was moving back and forth between the living creatures; it was bright, with lightning coming out of it. 14 The creatures were darting back and forth like flashes of lightning." (Ezek. 1: 5-14)

Have you ever wondered who these beasts are? What is their connection to the presence of God? There were four living creatures with four wings and four faces. The four faces were the man, lion, ox, and eagle, and they had hands like a man. Their legs were straight and their feet like a calf's hoof. Two wings of each one were touching the adjacent wing of the creatures on either side of it, and the two other wings of each creature covered its body. Wherever the Spirit would go they went as well.

> "When they moved, I heard the sound of their wings like the roar of mighty waters, like the voice of the Almighty, and a sound of commotion like the noise of an army. When they stood still, they lowered their wings." (Ezek. 1:24, HCSB)

WHEELS

There were wheels beside the living creatures. What are these wheels with eyes all over? Our finite mind cannot imagine. They were possibly the wheels to the throne of God. Ezekiel 1-10 gives us an insight into God's throne moving from the middle of the Sanctuary outward until He finally leaves the city. It is pretty simple - God is seated on His throne. The cherubim are His chariot-bearers, and the wheels are a part of His throne. When the throne is in heaven, there are no wheels mentioned. They are only mentioned when God's throne is seen moving on the earth.

> "[16] The appearance of the wheels and their craftsmanship was like the gleam of beryl, and all four had the same form. Their appearance and craftsmanship was like a wheel within a wheel. [17] When they moved, they went in any of the four directions, without pivoting as they moved. [18] Their rims were large and frightening. Each of their four rims were full of eyes all around. [19] So when the living creatures moved, the wheels moved beside them, and when the creatures rose from the earth, the wheels also rose. [20] Wherever the Spirit wanted to go, the creatures went in the direction the Spirit was moving. The wheels rose alongside them, for the spirit of the living creatures was in the wheels." (Ezek. 1:16 – 20, HCSB)

The cherubim move with the throne, and in heaven they are the sentinels before the throne.

FIRMAMENT

Over the heads of the living creatures was the likeness of a firmament, resembling a dazzling crystal or ice stretched across the sky.

> "Something like a sea of glass, similar to crystal, was also before the throne..."
> (Rev. 4:6, HCSB)

THRONE

The throne is above the firmament. Ezekiel 1:26 describes the shape of the throne as having the appearance of a sapphire stone. Seated above the likeness of a throne was a likeness with the appearance of a Man.

> "[3] and the One seated looked like jasper and carnelian stone. A rainbow that looked like an emerald surrounded the throne. [4] Around that throne were 24 thrones, and on the thrones sat 24 elders dressed in white clothes, with gold crowns on their heads. [5] Flashes of lightning and rumblings of thunder came from the throne. Seven fiery torches were burning before the throne, which are the seven spirits of God." (Rev. 4:3-5, HCSB)

What an awesome sight! God has the likeness of a Man, but Ezekiel cannot see His face because of the Glory that radiates from His Being. Weird wheels and cherubim with four faces? That awesome sight is a bit to take in, don't you think? The whole vision is mind-blowing, but He is the crux of everything the prophet sees.

THE ONE THAT SAT ON THE THRONE

> "²⁷ From what seemed to be His waist up, I saw a gleam like amber, with what looked like fire enclosing it all around. From what seemed to be His waist down, I also saw what looked like fire. There was a brilliant light all around Him. ²⁸ The appearance of the brilliant light all around was like that of a rainbow in a cloud on a rainy day. This was the appearance of the form of the Lord's glory. When I saw it, I fell facedown and heard a voice speaking." (Ezek. 1:27-28, HCSB)

> "...and the One seated looked like jasper and carnelian stone. A rainbow that looked like an emerald surrounded the throne." (Rev. 4:3, HCSB)

Ezekiel heard the voice of God when He commissioned him to serve as a prophet to the Israelites during the Babylonian captivity.

At the first reading of Ezekiel's vision, these outer space type elements in the vision may be intimidating or confusing. Don't get so caught up looking at the wheels and the cherubim that you miss the radiant One on the Throne! It is all about Him, this glorious God!

THRONE OF GLORY

"Listen, Shepherd of Israel, who leads Joseph like a flock; You who sit enthroned on the cherubim, rise up." (Ps. 80:1, HCSB)

"...the weight of refined gold for the altar of incense; and the plans for the chariot of the gold cherubim that spread out their wings and cover the ark of the Lord's covenant." (1 Chron. 28:18, HCSB)

CHERUBIM

The cherubim seen in the books of Ezekiel and Revelation are the guardians of the throne and accompany it wherever it goes.

"I called to the Lord in my distress, and I cried to my God for help. From His temple, He heard my voice and my cry to Him reached His ears. Then the earth shook and quaked; the foundations of the mountains trembled; they shook because He burned with anger. 8 Smoke rose from His nostrils, and consuming fire came from His mouth; coals were set ablaze by it. 9 He parted the heavens and came down, a dark cloud beneath His feet. 10 He rode on a cherub and flew, soaring on the wings of the wind. 11 He made darkness His hiding place, dark storm clouds His canopy around Him. 12 From the radiance of His presence, His clouds swept onward with hail and blazing coals. 13 The Lord thundered from heaven; the Most High projected His voice. 14 He shot His arrows and scattered them; He hurled lightning bolts and routed them." (Ps. 18:6-14, HCSB)

PARALLELS IN THE VISIONS OF EZEKIEL 1 AND PSALM 18

There are various similarities between the visions of Ezekiel 1 and Psalm 18. These include the sighting of fire and smoke, thick clouds, radiance, lightning, whirlwind, and coals.

ISAIAH'S VISION OF THE GLORY

Isaiah was a prophet during the reign of Kings Uzziah, Jotham, Ahaz, and Hezekiah. Some of these kings were good, but the people of Judah followed the practices of idolatrous Israel. God saw their sins were red as scarlet (Isa. 1:18) and that they did not know their master (Isa. 1:3). Verse 21 of Isaiah 1 talks about how the faithful city had become a harlot.

Hosea also prophesied alongside Isaiah. The prophet Hosea was commissioned in Hosea 1:2 to marry a promiscuous wife and have children of promiscuity . This was a portrayal of the nation of Israel committing spiritual promiscuity by abandoning the Lord.

God called Isaiah to be a prophet while Judah was in a state of moral decline. Just as Ezekiel at the time of his calling, God revealed His glory to the prophet.

> "In the year that King Uzziah died, I saw the Lord seated on a high and lofty throne, and His robe filled the temple. ²Seraphim were standing above Him; each one had six wings: with two he covered his face, with two he covered his feet, and with two he flew. ³ And one called to another: Holy, holy, holy is the Lord of Hosts; His glory fills the whole earth. ⁴ The foundations of the doorways shook at the sound of their voices, and the temple was filled with smoke. ⁵ Then I said: Woe is me for I am ruined because I am a man of unclean lips and live among a people of unclean lips, and because my eyes have seen the King, the Lord of Hosts." (Isa. 6:1-5, HCSB)

ELEMENTS OF ISAIAH'S VISION

Isaiah's vision talks about God seated on a high throne. His train filled the Temple, the posts were shaken and the house was full of smoke.

SERAPHIM

"The Seraphim have three pair of wings. They are the "attendants of the Lord of Hosts and call attention to His holiness."" (Larkin)[3]

The seraphim flying above the throne of God belong to the hierarchy of angels and have six wings. Their ministry is to call special attention to God's glory and majesty. Their main focus is the worship of God. Their eternal song in Isaiah 6:3 (HCSB) proclaims, "Holy, holy, holy is the LORD of Hosts; His glory fills the whole earth." Isaiah saw God's throne in the Temple, while Ezekiel saw Him leaving the Temple. What happened that caused God's glory to be driven from the Temple? Clearly, God did not like to leave His place of rest, so what prompted His departure?

EZEKIEL'S VISIONS

Ezekiel was the prophet to the Israelites who were captives in Babylon. Judah was ruled by a king who was a vassal to the Babylonians. Judah still had their city and temple . As far as they were concerned, God was with them while the temple was still standing. They did not realize that in their hearts they were far from Him. Between Isaiah and Ezekiel's time, Judah's spiritual adultery progressively grew more acute until they hardly knew God anymore. Ezekiel prophesied of the final downfall of Jerusalem. This was a physical result of God's glory departing due to Judah's unrepentant harlotry.

Jeremiah was Ezekiel's counterpart, who prophesied to the king and people in Judah. The book of Jeremiah speaks of the sin and downfall of Judah. While Ezekiel remained in Babylon, Jeremiah prophesied and witnessed the fall of Jerusalem. Jeremiah was eventually carried captive to Babylon after the city and temple were destroyed. Ezekiel 1 is the vision of the glory revealed to Ezekiel as he is called to be a prophet to the exiles in Babylon. What was the purpose and significance of this vision? Ezekiel experienced the desolation of the exiles and he saw the glory departing from the temple. He was also given visions of hope of the restoration of the nation of Israel and the rebuilding of a new temple where the glory of God would reside again.

A Timeline of Kings and Prophets

PROPHET	LOCATION	KING			
Hosea	Israel	Uzziah	Jotham	Ahaz	Hezekiah
Jeremiah	Judah	Josiah	Jehoahaz	Jehoaikim & Jehoaichin	Zedekiah
Ezekiel	Babylon	Josiah	Jehoahaz	Jehoaikim & Jehoaichin	Zedekiah

THE GLORY DEPARTS

In Ezekiel 8:1, the hand of the Lord was upon Ezekiel, and he saw the Lord. The Lord lifted him up by his hair and took him to Jerusalem in the visions of God.

> "³ He stretched out what appeared to be a hand and took me by the hair of my head. Then the Spirit lifted me up between earth and heaven and carried me in visions of God to Jerusalem, to the entrance of the inner gate that faces north, where the offensive statue that provokes jealousy was located. ⁴I saw the glory of the God of Israel there, like the vision I had seen in the plain.⁵ The Lord said to me, "Son of man, look toward the north." I looked to the north, and there was this offensive statue north of the altar gate, at the entrance." (Ezek. 8:3-5, HCSB)

What is wrong with this picture? The idol is situated in the inner court of the temple. It may have been placed there by King Manasseh. The altar had been fashioned by King Ahaz after the pattern of a pagan altar he had seen in another kingdom. The glory of God is in the inner court, not in the Holy of Holies, which is God's resting place.

> "He said to me, "Son of man, do you see what they are doing here, more detestable things that the house of Israel is committing, so that I must depart from My sanctuary? You will see even more detestable things."" (Ezek. 8:6, HCSB)

The prophet was next shown a hole in the wall of the court. When he dug into it, he found a doorway. God was showing him the hidden wickedness of Judah.

> "¹⁰I went in and looked, and there engraved all around the wall was every form of detestable thing, crawling creatures and beasts, as well as all the idols of the house of Israel. ¹¹Seventy elders from the house of Israel were standing before them, with Jaazaniah son of Shaphan standing among them. Each had a firepan in his hand, and a fragrant cloud of incense was rising up. ¹²Then He said to me, "Son of man, do you see what the elders of the house of Israel are doing in the darkness, each at the shrine of his idol? For they are saying, "The Lord does not see us. The Lord has abandoned the land." ¹³Again He said to me, "You will see even more detestable things, which they are committing." ¹⁴ So He brought me to the entrance of the north gate of the Lord's house, and I saw women there weeping for Tammuz." (Ezek. 8:10-14, HCSB)

An annual feast was celebrated to him in June (hence called Tammuz in the Jewish calendar) at Byblos, when the Syrian women, in wild grief, tore off their hair and yielded their persons to prostitution, consecrating the hire of their infamy to Venus; next followed days of rejoicing for his return to the earth – (Jamieson, Fausset & Brown)[4]

"[16] So He brought me to the inner court of the Lord's house, and there were about 25 men at the entrance of the Lord's temple, between the portico and the altar, with their backs to the Lord's temple and their faces turned to the east. They were bowing to the east in worship of the sun. [17] And He said to me, "Do you see this, son of man? Is it not enough for the house of Judah to commit the detestable things they are practicing here, that they must also fill the land with violence and repeatedly provoke Me to anger, even putting the branch to their nose?" (Ezek. 8:16-17, HCSB)

The Jews felt that God had disowned them and used this excuse to turn to other gods. They had in fact forsaken Him and they were driving God away from His place of rest by worshiping other deities.

Whenever God is not at the center of our lives or even in Jerusalem, everything begins to disintegrate. As people's hearts were going astray, their streets were pervaded with violence and dishonesty. Their actions were just the 'fruit' of their capricious hearts.

"Then He called to me directly with a loud voice, "Come near, executioners of the city, each of you with a destructive weapon in his hand." [2] And I saw six men coming from the direction of the Upper Gate, which faces north, each with a war club in his hand. There was another man among them, clothed in linen, with writing equipment at his side. They came and stood beside the bronze altar. [3] Then the glory of the God of Israel rose from above the cherub where it had been, to the threshold of the temple. He called to the man clothed in linen with the writing equipment at his side." (Ezek. 9:1-3, HCSB)

The glory of God was slowly moving away from His place of rest. The glory and cherubs had moved outwards from the Holiest Place to the inner court and was seen hovering over the threshold of the temple. God is long-suffering and merciful. This should have moved the Jews to repent, but they did not as they did not discern that glory had left. After this, the city was given over to destruction.

The six destroying angels (guards of the city) were sent to destroy all those who were not sealed. This is what happened in the spiritual realm. This destruction manifested in the natural realm when the Babylonians destroyed Judah.

"Then I looked, and there above the expanse over the heads of the cherubim was something like sapphire stone resembling the shape of a throne that appeared above them. [2] The Lord spoke to the man clothed in linen and said, "Go inside the wheelwork beneath the cherubim. Fill your hands with hot coals from among the cherubim and scatter them over the city." So he went in as I watched. [3] Now the cherubim were standing to the south of the temple when the man went in, and the cloud filled the inner court. [4] Then the glory of the Lord rose from above the cherub to the threshold of the temple. The temple was filled with the cloud, and the court was filled with the brightness of the Lord's glory." (Ezek. 10:1-4, HCSB)

THE GLORY DEPARTS FROM THE TEMPLE

"[18] Then the glory of the Lord moved away from the threshold of the temple and stood above the cherubim. [19] The cherubim lifted their wings and ascended from the earth right before my eyes; the wheels were beside them as they went. The glory of the God of Israel was above them, and it stood at the entrance to the eastern gate of the Lord." (Ezek. 10:18-19, HCSB)

THE GLORY DEPARTS FROM THE CITY

"[22] Then the cherubim, with the wheels beside them, lifted their wings, and the glory of the God of Israel was above them. [23] The glory of the LORD rose up from within the city and stood on the mountain east of the city." (Ezek. 11:22-23, HCSB)

This incident reminds me of the story of the Arab and the camel. The camel first asked for a bit of space in the Arab's tent. The camel encroached into the Arab's space a little at a time until the Arab was completely thrust out of his tent. Similarly, as God's people made room for wickedness, they slowly pushed God out of His rightful place and didn't know it!

GOD WANTS TO STAY

God hesitated to leave the temple. He never wanted to leave His place of rest. Sadly, He was driven away from it.

MAKE SPACE FOR GOD

We need to give God the central, most treasured space in our hearts, as He deserves this eminence. Other gods cannot take up residence beside Him. He will not share His glory with another. Remember the story of the humiliation of the idol Dagon and the Ark of God in 1 Sam 5?

The demon possessed man in the Gadarenes was possessed by a legion of 6,000 demons. This demonstrates that the human spirit has a great capacity. This is the mystery. The heavens cannot contain God, yet He chooses to dwell within us. Our bodies may be made of dust, but our spirits have been made to be the temple to house the Lord of Lords.

Consider the story of the widow whose sons were going to be taken away by the creditors. Elisha asked her to get as many vessels as possible. The limited quantity of oil that the widow had in her possession was multiplied. As long as there were crucibles to fill, the flow of oil continued. As soon as the vessels ran out, the flow ceased. We infer that God is willing to fill us with His glory as long as we are willing to make space for Him at the center of our hearts. When we thirst after God and pursue His Presence, we make space for Him. Our innermost being is the Holiest Place, the sanctum of the Most High and Lofty One. We must not give this place to anyone or anything.

GLORY ON THE MOUNTAIN

ADAM HID

In Genesis, Adam freely walked with God, and he was clothed with glory (*kabod*) and honor.

> "You made him little less than God and crowned him with glory and honor." (Ps. 8:5, HCSB)

Once he sinned, he hid from the presence of God.

> "Then the man and his wife heard the sound of the Lord God walking in the garden at the time of the evening breeze, and they hid themselves from the Lord God among the trees of the garden." (Gen. 3:8, HCSB)

The glory departed from him, and he saw that he was naked. He could not walk with God as before. Adam had to hide his sinful flesh from God because sin cannot stand before Him. From this time forward, man could not walk with God. Sin separates. Now man could only worship from afar.

Let us look at the instances where the Israelites experienced God's glory at Sinai.

MOSES AND ISRAEL

Moses was the mediator of the Old Covenant. God spoke to him and the people were glad to have a mediator as they feared the voice and glory of God. To make it worse a boundary was set to prevent people from approaching the mountain.

> "Put boundaries for the people all around the mountain and say: Be careful that you don't go up on the mountain or touch its base. Anyone who touches the mountain will be put to death." (Ex. 19:12, HCSB)

The glory of God consumes sinful flesh, unless there is a covering for it.

> "On the third day, when morning came, there was thunder and lightning, a thick cloud on the mountain, and a loud trumpet sound, so that all the people in the camp shuddered." (Ex. 19:16, HCSB)

> "The Lord came down on Mount Sinai at the top of the mountain. Then the Lord summoned Moses to the top of the mountain, and he went up." (Ex. 19:20, HCSB)

> "So Moses went down to the people and told them." (Ex. 19:25, HCSB)

The Ten Commandments were given by God to Moses, who in turn went down and relayed the commands to Israel.

> "All the people witnessed the thunder and lightning, the sound of the trumpet, and the mountain surrounded by smoke. When the people saw it they trembled and stood at a distance." (Ex. 20:18, HCSB)

Man had fallen so far from the glory that the sight of it caused them to move further away out of fear. The guilt and shame associated with sin will cause us to run away from God when we should be running towards His grace.

> "19You speak to us, and we will listen," they said to Moses, "but don't let God speak to us, or we will die." (Ex. 20:19, HCSB)

Man could not bear to hear the voice of God. They felt that they would be killed by the very voice that brought things to life. Moses was the mediator between a Holy God and estranged man.

> "And the people remained standing at a distance as Moses approached the thick darkness where God was." (Ex. 20:21, HCSB)

Man could not draw near to God. Sin tragically increased the distance between God and man. Thank God for the atoning efficacy of the blood of Christ that ushers us into His Presence. Hallelujah!

AARON, NADAB, ABIHU AND SEVENTY ELDERS

> "Then He said to Moses, "Go up to the Lord, you and Aaron, Nadab, and Abihu, and 70 of Israel's elders, and bow in worship at a distance. 2Moses alone is to approach the Lord, but the others are not to approach, and the people are not to go up with him." (Ex. 24:1-2, HCSB)

The Mosaic covenant was established. The book of the covenant was read and blood was sprinkled.

> "9 Then Moses went up with Aaron, Nadab, and Abihu, and 70 of Israel: 10and they saw the God of Israel. Beneath His feet was something like a pavement made of sapphire stone, as clear as the sky itself. 11God did not harm the Israelite nobles; they saw Him, and they ate and drank." (Ex. 24:9-11, HCSB)

They were not consumed, because they had been sprinkled by the blood of the Covenant. They are now eating and drinking in His Presence. Does this sound familiar? This is a shadow of blood-washed, New Testament saints taking communion.

> "15When Moses went up the mountain, the cloud covered it. 16The glory of the LORD settled on Mount Sinai, and the cloud covered it for six days. On the seventh day He

called to Moses from the cloud. ¹⁷ The appearance of the Lord's glory to the Israelites was like a consuming fire on the mountaintop." (Ex. 24:15-17, HCSB)

This scene represents people encountering God's glory at different levels. Moses was the closest in the cloud. Aaron and the others were invited to come up and behold the glory. Joshua waited at a lower level, while the people were at the base of the mountain afraid to come near to God. The sad part is that the people exchanged the Shekinah Glory for a golden calf. This is a perfect example of what the author of Romans was talking about.

"…and exchanged the glory of the immortal God for images resembling mortal man, birds, four-footed animals, and reptiles." (Rom. 1:23, HCSB)

How did the glory impact different people's lives? Moses continued to grow in fellowship with God. Aaron made a golden calf even after seeing God. Joshua lingered at the tabernacle even after Moses left, revealing his earnest desire for more of God. In Leviticus 10, Nadab and Abihu, the eldest sons of Aaron, offered strange fire, and a fire from the Lord devoured them because they did not revere God's glory. How does the glory of God affect you? Imagine if we sought God like Moses did.

SHOW ME YOUR GLORY

"¹⁸ Then Moses said, "Please, let me see Your glory." ¹⁹He said, "I will cause all My goodness to pass in front of you, and I will proclaim the name Yahweh before you. I will be gracious to whom I will be gracious, and I will have compassion on whom I will have compassion."²⁰ But He answered, "You cannot see My face, for no one can see Me and live." ²¹The Lord said, "Here is a place near Me. You are to stand on the rock, ²² and when My glory passes by, I will put you in the crevice of the rock and cover you with My hand until I have passed by. ²³Then I will take My hand away, and you will see My back, but My face will not be seen."" (Ex. 33:18-23, HCSB)

By this time, Moses was accustomed to dwelling in God's Presence. Unsatisfied, he dared to ask for more of God. Under the old covenant, man needed some form of covering to protect him from being consumed by the glory. Through the Bible, we see that no man ever saw God's face. Note that Moses stayed without food or water for 40 days. He was sustained by the glory of His presence. Please note that God granted Moses his request, as the scripture records that God spoke to Moses face to face.

"And there arose not a prophet since in Israel like unto Moses, whom the LORD knew face to face..." (Dt. 34:10, HCSB)

THE VEIL

"²⁹ As Moses descended from Mount Sinai – with the two tablets of the testimony in his hands as he descended the mountain – he did not realize that the skin of his face shone as a result of his speaking with the Lord. ³⁰ When Aaron and all the Israelites saw Moses, the skin of his face shone! They were afraid to come near him." (Ex. 34:29-30, HCSB)

When man falls out of fellowship with God, the thought of God brings fear, guilt, and judgement. Sin drives man away from His holiness. All God really wants is for us to draw near to Him. He will cleanse us and make us holy. We will find Him if we seek Him. He will not cast off anyone who comes to Him. This is the grace of the New Testament. The blood of Christ has been poured out on the mercy seat in heaven, God's judgment has been stayed on the person who believes and comes to God in repentance. Arise and shine, for the glory of the Lord will shine upon us.

> "³¹ But Moses called out to them, so Aaron and all the leaders of the community returned to him, and Moses spoke to them. ³²Afterward all the Israelites came near, and he commanded them to do everything the Lord had told him on Mount Sinai. ³³ When Moses had finished speaking with them, he put a veil over his face. ³⁴ But whenever Moses went before the Lord to speak with Him, he would remove the veil until he came out. After he came out, he would tell the Israelites what he had been commanded, ³⁵ and the Israelites would see that Moses' face was radiant. Then Moses would put the veil over his face again until he went to speak with the Lord." (Ex. 34:31-35, HCSB)

The letter kills. The ministry of the stone tablets brought death. This glory of the old covenant was fading away. We have been set free from the Law of Sin and Death and we now follow the Law of the Spirit of Life. The Holy Spirit will show us the glory of Jesus. Can you fathom the greater glory that we can experience under the new covenant? Don't settle for what everyone else experiences. There is always more of God for us to experience. We haven't seen anything yet.

GLORY OF THE ONLY BEGOTTEN

JESUS THE ONE AND ONLY

"The Word became flesh and took up residence among us. We observed His glory, the glory as the One and Only Son from the Father, full of grace and truth." (John 1:14, HCSB)

Can we see God? Can we behold and experience His glory? Or is it like in the Old Testament, when everyone fled from His awesomeness?

"No one has ever seen God. The One and Only Son – the One who is at the Father's side – He has revealed Him." (John 1:18, HCSB)

Jesus came to reconcile us to God, to return us to God and His glory. How can we experience so much of God?

"⁹But we do see Jesus—made lower than the angels for a short time so that by God's grace He might taste death for everyone—crowned with glory and honor because of His suffering in death. ¹⁰For in bringing many sons to glory, it was entirely appropriate that God—all things exist for Him and through Him—should make the source of their salvation perfect through sufferings." (Heb. 2:9-10, HCSB)

Man may have fallen from glory, but Christ has redeemed and restored 'many sons' back to the glory of God. We are no longer separated - there are no more boundaries because of the blood of Christ. Now the Holy Spirit gives us access to the Father.

TRANSFIGURATION

"After six days Jesus took Peter, James, and his brother John and led them up on a high mountain by themselves. ²He was transformed in front of them, and His face shone like the sun. Even His clothes became as white as the light." (Matt. 17:1-2, HCSB)

"⁵While He was still speaking, suddenly a bright cloud covered them, and a voice from the cloud said: This is My Beloved Son. I take delight in Him. Listen to Him! ⁶When the disciples heard it, they fell facedown and were terrified. ⁷Then Jesus came up, touched them, and said, "Get up; don't be afraid." (Matt. 17:5-7, HCSB)

At Sinai, the people were trembling with fear and stood afar off. Jesus has removed this fear that drives us away from God. He has drawn us to God by His blood and grace.

"All of a sudden, when the whole crowd saw Him, they were amazed and ran to greet Him." (Mark 9:15, HCSB)

People are running towards Jesus, not away from Him.

SINAI AND ZION

Sinai is a shadow of Zion. The law was given at Sinai, but Zion is a place of grace and truth. Sinai was an inapproachable place of gloom, judgement, terror, and trembling. We are now to come to Mt. Zion, a place of festive gathering and rejoicing. The blood of Jesus speaks life on our behalf, and we can approach God without fear of death. Continue to reverence the God of Zion, and don't lose sight of His grace.

> "28Therefore, since we are receiving a kingdom that cannot be shaken, let us hold on to grace. By it, we may serve God acceptably, with reverence and awe, 29for our God is a consuming fire." (Heb. 12:28-29, HCSB)

BEHOLDING THE GLORY

We are a Christ's letter, engraved on the tablets of our heart by the Spirit of God. The glory associated with the Law was fading away. How much more glorious is the ministry of the Spirit?

> "9 For if the ministry of condemnation had glory, the ministry of righteousness overflows with even more glory. 10 In fact, what had been glorious is not glorious now by comparison because of the glory that surpasses it. 11 For if what was fading away was glorious, what endures will be even more glorious." (2 Cor. 3:9-11, HCSB)

If there is so much more glory, why don't we experience it? There has to be more. When the Spirit anoints the word and reveals Jesus to us, we will experience His glory.

> "16 ... but whenever a person turns to the Lord, the veil is removed. 17 Now the Lord is the Spirit, and where the Spirit of the Lord is, there is freedom. 18 We all, with unveiled faces, are looking as in a mirror at the glory of the Lord and are being transformed into the same image from glory to glory; this is from the Lord who is the Spirit." (2 Cor. 3:3-18, HCSB)

The Glory will only be revealed to us through the Holy Spirit. Jesus has declared the Father to us. We no longer need to fear as did the Israelites. As we dwell in His Word and behold the beauty of Christ, we will be changed by the Spirit of the Lord into His image with ever-increasing glory. The word 'transformed' is the same word used to describe metamorphosis. We can only be changed by beholding His glory. Only when we make the Holy Spirit Lord will we experience the liberty He promises.

Mt. Sinai vs. Mt. Zion

SINAI	ZION
Cannot be approached or touched	We have come
Moses the mediator	Jesus the mediator
Old covenant	New covenant
Lamb's blood	Jesus' blood
Adam's blood speaks vengeance	Jesus' blood speaks redemption and forgiveness
Terror drove people away	People are drawn to Jesus
God is a consuming fire – trembling and fear	Consuming fire- reverence and awe
Tablets of stone written by finger of God	Tablets of human heart written by Spirit
Letter kills, brought death	Spirit gives life
Glory fading away	Surpassing glory that lasts
Veil of Moses on hearts	Unveiled face behold the Lord's glory

> "Why then was the law given? It was added because of transgressions until the Seed to whom the promise was made would come. The law was put into effect through angels by means of a mediator." (Gal. 3:19, HCSB)

God shielded Moses with his hand. Jesus' grace shields us today. His blood, name, and the fact that He is the mediator of the new covenant has brought us (many sons) into glory. Only when we receive our glorified bodies will we be able to completely experience His glory.

> "In fact, what had been glorious is not glorious now by comparison because of the glory that surpasses it." (2 Cor. 3:10, HCSB)

The glory of the Old Testament was fading away, making way for the glory of Jesus which excels. Can you even fathom that we can be part of this picture? Christ in us is the hope of glory.

GLOSSARY

Abba: Aramaic equivalent of the Hebrew word 'Father'

Abrek: an Egyptian word meaning 'Attention' or a Hebrew word for 'Kneel'

Addereth: Glory or Cloak

Addereth: Hebrew word for an Outer Garment

Beer : Hebrew word for Well

Beer-lahai-roi: Hebrew for The well of the Living One who sees me or The well of Him that lives and sees me

Boaz: Hebrew word for 'in its strength'; The name of the left of two pillars in Solomon's temple

Bene: Hebrew word for Understanding, Discern, Understand, Consider

Charis: Greek word for Grace, Favor, Kindness, Divine Grace

Charismata: Hebrew word for Spiritual Gifts

Charisms: Hebrew word for Special or Extraordinary Power (as of healing)

Chazown: Hebrew word for Vision, Oracle, Prophecy; Divine Communication

Checked: Hebrew word for Goodness, Kindness, Faithfulness

Chen: Hebrew word for Favor, Grace

Divan: Persian word for a Long low sofa without a back or arms, typically placed against a wall

Dunamis: Greek word for Strength, Power, Ability. Inherent power residing in a thing by virtue of its nature, or which a person or thing exerts and puts forth

El Roi: Hebrew for The Living One who sees me

Esek: Hebrew word for Quarrel, Contention; Name of a well which Isaac's herdsmen dug in the valley of Gerar

Ga'al: Hebrew word for Redeem or Act as kinsman

Gada: Hebrew word for to hew or chop down

Ginosko: Greek word for Get a knowledge of, Understand; Godly wisdom in contrast to earthly wisdom and experience

Jachin: Hebrew word for 'Yah will establish'; The name of the right of two pillars in Solomon's temple

Kabod: Hebrew word for Glory of God, Weighty or heavy presence of God

Khakam: Hebrew word for Human wisdom, Know by experience

Logos: Greek word for the inspired written word of God; also refers to Jesus who is the Living Word

Mashakh: Hebrew word for anointing, which is smearing or spreading a liquid

Meheel: Hebrew word for Common outer cloak or garment

Meshiyach: Hebrew word for The Anointed one

Metamorphoo: Greek word for transformation or transfiguration

Paga: Fountain or Spring

Para: Hebrew word for Let loose, Be loosened of restraint, Make unbridled, or to reveal

Parabola: Greek word for a Placing of one thing beside another, juxtaposition, Comparison of one thing to another, Likeness, Similitude, Parable, an Earthly story with a heavenly meaning

Parakletos: Greek word for Advocate or Helper, Pleader, Succorer, Aider, Assistant

Pentecost: Greek word for Fifty

Pneuma: Greek word for Spirit, Wind, or Breath

Pneumatikos: Greek word for Spiritual Man

Psyche: Hebrew word for the Soul

Psychikos: Greek word for Sensual, Soulish, Fleshly, Carnal

Reheboth: Hebrew word for Spaciousness, Wide places; Name of a well dug by Isaac in the valley of Gerar

Rhema: Greek word for the Illumination or quickening of a specific scripture that applies directly to our personal situation; as distinguished from *logos,* the written Word of Gods

Sarkikos: Greek word for Carnal Man

Semikiyah: Hebrew word for Rug

Sheol: Greek word for underworld, grave or the abode of the dead

Sitnah: Hebrew word for Enmity, Hostility, Strife, Hatred; Name of a well dug by Isaac in the valley of Gerar

Soma: Hebrew word for the body

Yada - Hebrew word that means know by experience

Yahweh: A form of the Hebrew name of God used in the Bible

Yakar: Hebrew word for something valuable, prized, weighty, precious, rare, or splendid

Yatab: Hebrew word for good, well, glad, or pleasing

Yattiyr - Hebrew word for preeminent, surpassing, extreme, extraordinary, or very great

Yether: Hebrew word for abundance, affluence, preeminence, or that which exceeds measure or limit

Zoe: Greek word for Life

BIBLIOGRAPHY / REFERENCES

1. Dake, Finis J. "Notes on James 2:13". In *Dake's Annotated Reference Bible,* p. 261. Lawrenceville: Dake Bible Sales., 27th printing, April 1998.

2. Jamieson, Fausset & Brown, "Commentary on 1 Corinthians 12 by Jamieson, Fausset & Brown." Blue Letter Bible. Last Modified 19 Feb, 2000.
   https://www.blueletterbible.org//Comm/jfb/1Cr/1Cr_012.cfm

3. Larkin, Clarence. 1918. *Dispensational Truth or God's Plan and Purposes in the Ages.* Philiadelphia: Rev. Clarence Larkin Est.

4. Jamieson, Fausset & Brown, . "Commentary on Ezekiel 8 by Jamieson, Fausset & Brown." Blue Letter Bible. Last Modified 19 Feb, 2000. https://www.blueletterbible.org/Comm/jfb/Eze/Eze_008.cfm

Printed in the United States
By Bookmasters